CISTERCIAN STUDIES SERIES: NUMBER ONE HUNDRED SIXTY-THREE

THE CALL OF SILENT LOVE

Other Carthusian books by the same editor:

The Way of Silent Love (1993)
The Wound of Love (1994)

CISTERCIAN STUDIES SERIES: NUMBER ONE HUNDRED SIXTY-THREE

THE CALL OF SILENT LOVE

Carthusian Novice Conferences
II. VOCATION AND DISCERNMENT

by
a Carthusian

Translated by
an Anglican Solitary

Cistercian Publications
Kalamazoo, Michigan

First published in 1995 by
Darton, Longman and Todd Ltd
London

and

Cistercian Publications Inc
WMU Station
Kalamazoo, Michigan 49008

Distribution:

Cistercian Publications Inc
St Joseph's Abbey
167 North Spencer Road
Spencer, MA 01562–1233

ISBN 0 87907 663 1

The work of Cistercian Publications is made possible in part
by support from Western Michigan University to
The Institute of Cistercian Studies

In joyful welcome and gratitude
to all Carthusians in heart.

Contents

Acknowledgement

The Translator gratefully acknowledges the assistance of
a Sister of the Community of St Clare
who checked the translation against the French original
and whose invaluable suggestions
almost invariably have been incorporated.

1

Bruno: A Time, a Place, a Man

First, let us have a panoramic overview of the life of Bruno, with whom you are familiar in any event.

About 1028: birth and early education at Cologne, Germany.

A. *Active Life* 1043–76 – thirty-three years:
life of study, then teaching and service in the Church in the cathedral schools of Rheims
  1043: student at fifteen years of age
        assistant professor
        canon of cathedral Chapter
  1056: *écolâtre*, that is, principal and rector of the university for twenty years
  1069 or 1070:
        chancellor of the cathedral
        dispute with the Archbishop of Rheims, Manasseh
        denunciation by the latter to the papal legate

B. *Transition* 1076–80 – four years:
  1076: stripped by Manasseh of his office and property
        takes refuge with Count Ebal de Ronci
        vows to leave the world for monastic life
  1080: Manasseh's deposition: Bruno potential arch bishop
        Bruno renounces everything

C. *Contemplative Life* 1080–1101 – twenty-one years:
  1081–4 – four years

experiment with eremitical life at
Sèche-Fontaine with two companions
1084–90 – six years
foundation in the mountains of the Chartreuse
(Bruno and six companions: four clerics (one
priest and two converse brothers)
1090–1101 – eleven years
Urban II calls Bruno to Rome as a counsellor.
He obeys, and stays several months. But his
companions break up and then regroup. He follows the Pope, who is driven to southern Italy.
Foundation of Santa Maria della Torre in
Calabria
1099: letter to Raoul le Verd and to his brothers in the
Charterhouse
1101: profession of faith, death

Thirty-three years of active life – a career in itself. Twenty-
five years of contemplative life. A new lease of life. Four
transitional years between the first and second ways of living.
He suffers a certain violence, in which we can discern God's
providence.

Who is Bruno? The information available to us is sparse,
those precious personal details that make up a living face.
Bruno speaks little of himself. The two personal letters of
his that we have use formal language and are stylised,
although they are very warm. In his time there was a different
sort of awareness of personality, but how much of this stylis-
ation is peculiar to Bruno and how much due to his context
is unknown.

Nonetheless, we have the broad outlines of his life, enough
to extract a solid and powerful figure as Houdon's statue
portrays him. Going to the essential, it portrays rather the
contemplative, the hermit, than Bruno as an individual; it is
no less true, though a little too 'perfect'. He lacks shadows.

We would love Bruno more spontaneously if we knew more of his struggles – even of his weaknesses – from inside.

Any effort to grasp his subjective experience more accurately, starting from the fragments of information we have, bears the imprint of the sensibility of the person who seeks to understand him. Inevitably, we project on him. Even so, it is worth the risk. For us who are called to the same vocation, the resonances of our heart meet those of Bruno's life and can help us sense his spirit.

At the same time, it is significant that Bruno escapes our curiosity. By vocation he is hidden in the secret of God. The features of his face are marked with divine light. The mystery that surrounds his person speaks more eloquently than his words. He did not write a rule of life, but he lived something so true and so profound that it is a source of fecundity still bearing new fruit in our day, not only in the Carthusian Order, but in all who claim him as their source, for example, the Brothers and Sisters of Bethlehem.

A TIME

A century of iron, said an historian of the eleventh century. The iron of the sword, the rule of the strongest, whose power is frequently in the service of greed. Church and Empire were engaged in mortal combat. It was a question of life and death for the Church to liberate itself from the intervention of secular powers in the appointment of its ministers, its bishops, even of the pope himself, and from the subordination of spiritual goods to temporal interests.

The struggle between Emperor Henry IV and Pope Gregory Hildebrand both symbolises and summarises what was at stake. On the one hand, councils of reform, severe self-criticism imposed on prelates, affirmation of liberty and of autonomy from the intrusion of princes into the spiritual realm, and on the other, wars, invasions and anti-councils, anti-popes, schism. The Church was in a period of grave crisis.

But it was also a period of great religious vitality. There was a return to the sources, and, faced with the spectacle of a Church mired in the venality of the world, people made radical choices. All Christian renewal expresses itself by an exodus into the desert. That is its law. As in the age of Constantine, many people sought the radical purification of solitude that brought them face to face with God. The Benedictine world demonstrated its vigour in its diverse reforms (the Cluniac, above all). The new orders of the Cistercians and the Camaldolese pressed the demands of poverty and solitude. Everywhere hermits established themselves in forests and lonely places. Not since the early days of the monastic life in Egypt had there been seen such an abundance of solitaries! Frequently, in the course of time, they ended by becoming absorbed by the communities near which they lived, more or less Benedictine or Cistercian.

Bruno's choice is more easily understood in this context. His is not an isolated case, an innovation. There are at least sixty-five instances of such experiments in the eleventh century. The only thing that distinguishes it from the others is its durability. A grain of life buried in the earth of solitude and silence, in an act of lively faith, in the fecundity of the eternal Cross, and in the primacy of God's action over human action, of the spiritual over the material. God first, and his Kingdom. The rest . . . the logic of love. It is even more remarkable that in founding a little hermitage in the Chartreuse, he never had any intention of founding an order. After the cathedral built by men, the one built by God, the desert: Sèche-Fontaine, the Chartreuse, Calabria. Let us talk about the Chartreuse, since we are here.

THE CHARTREUSE

The valley is narrow and has something of the clear sightlines of a cathedral nave about it: a vault of light encased within steep walls rising 1000 metres like arms outstretched in prayer.

The first hermitage was built at a spot higher up the valley, in the sanctuary. Great trees upheld the vault of heaven. Water poured from a crystal fountain. The incense of smoke from wood fires rose slowly. The small sounds of the natural world only enhanced the silence, an attentive listening to all that is. A place of prayer, a place of God. One could not live there without being marked by the One who dwells there.

A PLACE

For thirty-three years, the span of the life of Jesus, Bruno was a man of one of the most magnificent cathedrals in France – or in Europe, for that matter: the cathedral of Rheims, where French kings were crowned for centuries. Student, canon, professor, rector, chancellor – what powerful influence this place had on his spirit. Christian tradition at once intensely alive and translated into stone and the colours that embellished it. The presence of a single spirit, a crucified truth of unbroken continuity, the presence throughout time of a spirit, of a truth, of a whole world. The message of its teaching was simply the voice of these stones, of these realities which do not pass away. One cannot live in a place with impunity. The place moulds us in its own image, informs our imagination, inhabits our sensibility. Bruno's faith is heavy with mysteries that only symbols can evoke. Is this the secret of the harmony of proportion that we sense in this figure of Bruno, the harmony that makes him a little impersonal and 'sculptural'? The secret of this something of

serenity and nobility in his words and the evenness of his
disposition ... *semper vultu festo*, 'always with joyful face'?
His humanity is rooted like a great tree in the worldly and
incarnate reality of the Church of the Word of God. How
we need people of his contemplative weight to stabilise the
volatile Church!

THE MAN

A don, a distinguished professor, accustomed to living in an
intellectual atmosphere and an elevated social level and with
certain material comforts. He did not make a major contri-
bution to theology (as did, for example, St Anselm in the
same era); his writings, if there were any, have not survived
– the commentaries on the Psalms and on St Paul formerly
attributed to him do not seem to be from his hand. The
early age at which he became a professor suggests exceptional
intellectual qualities. The respect and reputation he enjoyed
seem to indicate teaching ability and great soundness of
learning. He had become a bulwark for tradition rather than
a speculative mind. The voice of the stones. Everything about
Bruno breathes balance and wise moderation.

The dispute with Manasseh and his detachment from the
responsible positions he exercised give a glimpse of his integrity and high moral stance. He was not one to exploit. His
integrity, accompanied by strength of character, made Bruno
capable of overcoming the obstacles and dangers attendant
on the position he took up. He showed himself to be steadfast
and exacting towards others, for example, with his friend
Raoul le Verd, with whom he seems a little severe and even
authoritarian.

All of this excellence is tempered by a warm affectivity,
concern for others, a capacity for tenderness. People
depended on him.

Bruno had the qualities of a leader, but if people followed him it was because they were led by their heart. He had the gift of friendship. His love of solitude was not misanthropy. Throughout his journey, from the decision made in Adam's garden to his death in Calabria, we find him always surrounded by friends. The first group at the Chartreuse is so organised around his person that panic and dispersal follow on his departure for Rome after six years of common life. Bruno was more than a friend, he was the master, the father. However, they gathered themselves together after a few months and the reassembled group made a fresh start under Lanuin, even though his role was a different one. Bruno remained the father, though absent. Meanwhile, the group had to take responsibility for its own life. It is interesting to speculate whether Bruno's departure might not have been a catalyst for maturation of the primitive group that enabled it to have a more egalitarian structure in its governance. Bruno's presence could have maintained too great a dependence. Who knows? In any case, it is curious that the group that formed around Bruno in Calabria and that benefited from his presence for eleven years did not turn out so well. Very quickly, Carthusian life was abandoned for a more communal life, it seems, because its identity was not sufficiently firmly established.

Bruno, then, exercised a profound influence over others; we can regard him as a spiritual master. He did not transmit more or less esoteric techniques. The structure of the life he lived with his companions is drawn from the classical monastic tradition: hermitages grouped after the fashion of a Palestinian lavra of the early centuries, a solitude in reality, but with the reinforcement of a common life on the one hand, and, on the other, certain liturgical offices in common each day. Their piety was fed by the common resources of the Church: the liturgy, the sacraments, the Word of God,

Christ. Their silence was not mute but resounded with celebration and the praise of God.

All his life, Bruno remained a man of the Church; he lived its life, he was moulded by its substance and shared its broad perspective. The service to speech of his early period was followed by the service to silence of a man of prayer. There was, at the same time, both continuity and rupture. On his deathbed he made an ecclesial profession of faith. It was in the name of his fidelity to the Church that he was opposed to the infamous archbishop – but what a crisis of conscience this must have been for this man who had such respect for ecclesiastical authority!

If he twice escaped the responsibility of high office in the Church and retired to the desert, it was only better to serve it, but by other means – prayer, sacrifice, the adoration of God alone. When the pope called him to his service, he did not hesitate to sacrifice his work, even though it seemed likely that it would not survive his absence.

It was the Church that led him to God and that fired him with the desire to see God's face. Over and above the inmost disposition of his mind, of his entire personality, intellectual, cultural, aesthetic, that the Church had effected in him, it also had given him its final secret, the thirst for God, for the presence of the Spirit and eternal life. 'That they may know you, the only true God, and Jesus Christ whom you have sent' (John 17:3).

This desire was maturing in the heart of the professor and the canon of Rheims during those long years. A balanced man, with depth of heart, integrity, never carried away. A long time had to pass so that this desire's mysterious way of renouncing human means, so noble in themselves, impressed itself upon him as the way to be followed. Christ only reveals his secrets slowly. Bruno would be a man fifty years old before he found the way to enter the paschal mystery of Christ.

Bruno was so completely immersed in his role of professor and chancellor that perhaps it took the extraordinary circumstances of his struggle with Archbishop Manasseh and his escape to the castle of Count Ebal de Ronci to effect the essential break.

The solitude of the first four years was an enforced solitude, not chosen, the leisure of an outlaw. The ties to his positions of honour and his possessions were brutally broken and exposed as worthless. In Bruno's two letters, he insistently returns to the theme of the vacuity of the world, compared with eternal joys. The crucial time in the moment of choice, as he tells us, was thus:

> In your affection you will remember the day when we met in the little garden adjoining the house of Adam, where I was then staying – you and I and Fulcius. We had been speaking for some time, if I remember rightly, of the false joys and deceitful riches of this world, comparing them with the eternal joys of heaven. You will recall how, while we talked, our hearts were burning with divine love, and we promised and even vowed that we would take the holy habit of religion as soon as possible and, fleeing for the future the shadows of this world, seek only those enduring joys of heaven.

'Burning with divine love . . .' The circumstances were only the catalyst for an acute perception of values in the light of the unique Good. Bruno's central intuition seemed to be a profound perception of the essential graciousness of God (but how can we talk of this? Everything carries the 'weight' of this word, 'God') and the joyous absorption, adoration, love that it entails. '*O Bonitas.*'

Bruno saw a life dedicated to the contemplation of God, not as a sacrifice that impoverished, but as the one thing most useful for a human being, the response to our deepest and most real needs (see the Letter to Raoul).

'Our hearts are restless until they rest in God' (Augustine). Bruno described to his friend Raoul the profound joys of a life thus in harmony with the truth of the human heart. He wrote his letters at the end of his life; they overflow with serene joy, the refulgence of peace and transparent wisdom. The contemplative life truly effects a foretaste of heaven.

> *Est, videt, amat:*
> *in aeternitate Dei viget*
> *in veritate Dei lucet*
> *in bonitate Dei gaudet.*

> He is, he sees, he loves:
> the eternity of God is his life,
> the truth of God is his light,
> the goodness of God is his joy.[1]

2

The Statutes

These Statutes contain, in renewed and adaptive form, the rule of life of our Fathers; to this rule let our hearing be attentive and on it let our meditation be continual: let us not forsake it and it will keep us, let us love it and it will guard us. For it is both the form and the sacrament of that holiness to which each of us has been predestined by God. (Statutes 4. 35. 1)[1]

The Statutes lay out for us a way that will lead us to God. We need to be acquainted with them in depth. We ought to study them, particularly in the course of the first year of the novitiate, as well as the Carthusian tradition and the monastic tradition in general. To help us, this series of conferences will develop the most essential themes of the Statutes and comment on some matters of practical interest.

We are not studying the Statutes as archaeologists. It is important to know the history of our Order to imbibe its spirit, but we must not stop there. It is a matter of making them alive for us, here and now. The essence of a religious observance resides in its inmost truth and in its fruits. It is in disposing ourselves to listen to the Spirit of God who has drawn us, in our turn, to his intimate love in solitude, that we read this text. It will help us better to lay bare the secret attraction of our heart, and teach us the appropriate response in the reality of life.

This knowledge should not remain merely speculative. We must question ourselves about the inmost truth with regard to each aspect of our life: are we truly living it out consciously and freely in our heart, and not as an outward constraint? And its fruits: does it help us to love God and our neighbour? Can we really fulfil them in the nitty-gritty of everyday life? How? (Statutes 4. 35. 4)

After each chapter, we will discuss together our reactions to the observance in question: how do we stand in relation to it and how can it help us live the life?

A LIVING TRADITION

It is not the text of the Statutes as such that interests us so much as the religious experience from which it is born. We are drinking in a tradition which, like the Gospel, was a living reality before being consigned to a text. It is only forty-three years (1084–1127) after the foundation of the Chartreuse by Bruno that Guigo, the fifth Prior, set down in writing the customs of the life that was being led there; and this on the insistence of other foundations that wanted to follow the same way of life, and not because there was a need to codify the observance. Guigo's Customs do not give a theory of Carthusian life; they simply record the way of life of the first Carthusians, practical wisdom about spiritual and mystical life. For the rest, Guigo sends us back to the monastic tradition.

We are inheritors of a living tradition, handed on from one to another down the centuries, incarnated in the reality of the lives of monks who lived in these same places, generation after generation. They were inspired by the same faith, they sought the same God, they prayed with the same words, chanted the same melodies, and doubtless suffered the same trials. The last link is the generation that has preceded us. We see in them the expression of the tradition of our fathers.

This immediate contact is very important. The transmission of a tradition is not accomplished only by the handing down of doctrines and practices. It is also done, perhaps, in the first place, by a kind of symbiosis. It is a life that is transmitted, and the breast that nourishes the younger members of a community on its substance is the concrete milieu of this living community. There is much that is communicated by means other than words. The reality is much greater than what is written down and what we are able to learn by reading the texts. We must therefore guard against too bookish an approach to Carthusian life. It is a life to be lived. It is a little like the relationship between holy Scripture and the living tradition of the Church, which alone assures its correct interpretation.

It is evident that, as in the larger Church, each generation is more or less faithful to the tradition and more or less selective. This or that aspect is more emphasised, such and such an observance more or less practised, according to the circumstances of the age and the action of grace. Incumbent on each generation is the task of assimilating the tradition, perhaps of deepening it. This is our responsibility also. Let us be very aware that we can only climb higher on the shoulders of our fathers.[2] We are the beginners. The way marked by our fathers has been proven for nine centuries. We feel the same inspiration as they did. Let us enter their school with humility and docility.

Let us not be satisfied with external conformity. Let us question ourselves continually: are we men of prayer like them? men of great love, men of faith? Do we have poverty, humility, simplicity, like them? Is our solitude fruitful?

THE ORIGIN OF THE STATUTES

Carthusian observance is not static. The motto '*numquam reformata*', 'never reformed', that we display with such insist-

ence does not imply a written law that has never changed
from its inception. Rather, what we see is a living organism
that constantly adapts itself to changing circumstances,
interior and exterior. Guigo's Customs were augmented six
times in the first 150 years, so that it was necessary to make
a compilation in 1271 that took the name *Antiqua Statuta*.[3]
These additions contained the decisions taken by the General Chapter that were of general interest. For the most part,
these were concrete cases of adaptation to the needs of the
life and expansion of the Order. Periodically it was necessary
to make further compilations. In 1368 the *Nova Statuta*, in
1509 the *Tertia Compilatio*, in 1582 the *Nova Collectio* which,
after the Council of Trent, brought together all the previous
compilations. In 1924 the *Statuta* were published: a revision
of the rule to comply with the new code of Canon Law
promulgated in 1917. In 1971 the first four books and in
1975 the last four books of the *Statuts Rénovés* (*Renewed
Statutes*) saw the light of day in the wake of the Second
Vatican Council.

VATICAN II

After the Council, the Order, along with all institutes of
religious, undertook the task of renewing its Statutes, as
mandated by the decrees of the Council. Everything that was
out of date was to be suppressed: for example, everything
that was juridically oppressive in the Order, liturgical
accretions that had been interpolated into the primitive
observance over the course of centuries. Certain liturgical
adaptations were made, and enriched with biblical and
patristic readings.

The style of the Statutes was also somewhat modified. In
general, they had been content to limit themselves to the
level of exterior observance. The Renewed Statutes – albeit

very discreetly – bring to light the scriptural and spiritual foundations of our life, above all amplifying the text by quotations from the Carthusian tradition (Bruno, Guigo, etc.) and from monastic tradition, especially from the East, thus establishing contact with the main sources of our life.

There were also the new or revised conciliar perspectives to incorporate: for example, on the subject of the way in which authority is exercised and the practice of obedience, with all that concerns relations among persons; the recognition by the Statutes of the full monastic status of the brothers, and the closer unity between the fathers in the cloister and the brothers; a greater awareness of the Church and of the function of the Order in the mystical Body of Christ. At the same time, the Council confirmed us most emphatically in our purely contemplative vocation. One only has to read the letter *Optimam Partem* that Pope Paul VI addressed to Reverend Father in 1971 in regard to renewal.[4] 'The contemplative life belongs to the fullness of the presence of the Church . . . Contemplation and continual prayer ought to be considered as primordial functions, which profit the entire universe.'

CREATIVE FIDELITY

The Customs of Guigo were conceived for a small group of men. The three centuries that ensued saw the birth and expansion of a great Order. By the sixteenth century there were 195 houses. And what social and religious upheavals between the twelfth and twentieth centuries! The Black Death, the great schism, the Protestant Reformation, the Counter-Reformation, the French Revolution, the suppression of the Order and the diaspora of the monks, the return and renaissance of the Order in 1817; then a second expulsion and exile in Italy, the First World War, the return in 1940, the Second World War, Vatican II, the present world crisis.

Inevitably, many changes and adaptations became imperative. But what is astonishing, truly astonishing, is the continuity of tradition, the fidelity of successive generations to an ideal that remained unchanged and a way of life whose essential elements were always the same. The reason for this, perhaps, is the extreme simplicity of our life, and a certain flexibility in regard to what is only secondary and subject to variation in each era. Even more, an excellent system of self-government through the Reverend Father, General Chapters and Visitors kept the principles of life of the early days from becoming deformed. This continual 'reform' avoided periodic disjunctive reforms that marked the history of so many religious orders.

This fidelity was not maintained by a mechanical repetition of what had gone before. It was a creative fidelity. It was a question of a spiritual reality, the search for God in solitude and in brotherhood, and each generation had to discover for itself the spirit of the vocation. Each generation has to live this adventure according to its truth (for us, as people of the twentieth century) and with a constant and ever deeper return to the sources,[5] drawing on St Bruno, Guigo, the Chartreuse in the primitive freshness of its vision, and in its saints across the centuries. A return to the sources also in the great monastic tradition, Western and Eastern. Above all from profound encounter with the Word of God in holy Scripture. Our life is no more than a response to this creative Word. It is in our being 'guided by the Gospel' that we go to the Father. 'But it is the Spirit who gives life, and he does not allow us to rest content with the mere letter; for to this alone these Statutes tend, that, guided by the Gospel, we may walk in the way of God and learn the breadth of love' (Statutes 4. 35. 1).

THE LETTER AND THE SPIRIT

The problem of the letter and the spirit is a very general one, not to betray the spirit and life through the paradigms in which they have taken shape – above all when these are effective. The means can obscure and displace the end. Something which served as an expression of an adventure, full of audacity, can become a protective wall against the challenge presented by faith and life.

Let us be suspicious of the temptation to stop at the letter of our Statutes. Yes, the letter is important, but only to the extent that it bears the spirit that upholds and expresses it. Let us also avoid the other extreme. There is a profound dialogue between the letter and the spirit. They are not set in opposition. Each needs the other. The spirit that does not take flesh risks being a mere illusion. And the house needs a framework. Sometimes it is the letter almost entirely on its own which assures continuity of the tradition, and which sustains an openness to the spirit of a more favourable time. This was the case in the nineteenth century after the almost total destruction of the Order by the French Revolution, when it had virtually to begin again from square one.

The ideal solution to the letter–spirit tension is to interiorise the values envisioned by the rule, that is to say, to embrace and make them our own, consciously and personally; to establish the observance within as a demand of our own unique spiritual life. Thus the difficulties of letter–spirit and law–liberty may be bypassed, because the law becomes the expression and support of my liberty. No one can compel me to do what I want to do. This is the singular situation with evangelical freedom, which is not a rejection of all law – St Paul says, 'Christ is my law' – but the law interiorised, written on our hearts, as the prophets foretold (Jeremiah 31:33). Such is the liberty in the Spirit of a child of God: the freedom that comes from love, the freedom that frees us

to love (Statutes 4. 35. 7). Conversely, without love, everything is worthless. 'For if life with Christ and intimate union
of the soul with God were lacking, faithfulness to ceremonies
and regular observance would be of little profit, and our life
could be justly compared to a body without a soul' (Statutes
1. 9. 5).

Of course in the beginning we have to accept a certain
number of prescriptions that do not correspond with our
interior spontaneity. This has a formative effect. With time
and experience we learn to enter more deeply and interiorly
into the observance, which culminates in a healthy liberty of
spirit. Liberty has its own course of development. It has to
be educated. The observance helps and liberates us from the
constraints of our egoism, of our sensuality, of our pride. It
is those who are led by the Spirit of God – by Love – who
are children of God.

APPENDIX

1084	Foundation of the Hermitage at Chartreuse
1090	Calabria
1127	*Guigo's Customs* (9 houses)
1140	Foundation of the Order: first General Chapter
	6 supplements to the Customs: 1140, 1170, 1180,
	1222, 1248
1271	*Antiqua Statuta*
	(compilation of the 6 supplements and Guigo's
	Customs)
1349	Black Death (900 victims)
1378	The Great Schism in the West:
	Order divided, 2 Reverend Fathers until 1409
	Two supplements (*Nova Statuta* 1368, *Tertia Com-*
	pilatio 1509)
	Just before the Protestant Reformation: 195 houses

1500–1600 Wars of Religion
(40 houses disappeared)
1582 *Nova Collectio* (after Trent)

(*Cells in the Grande Chartreuse: 12 in 1126, 20 in 1324, 24 in 1338, 35 in 1595*)

17th Century
Population explosion (555 professed at the Grande Chartreuse, 94.6% perseverance)
1675–1703 Le Masson is Reverend Father – Order: 16 Provinces; in France, 66 houses
160 houses total

18th Century
Joseph II of Austria suppresses 24 houses
1789 French Revolution, confiscation of Church property
1792 Suppression of religious institutes, diaspora of monks

19th Century
1805 Only a few Charterhouses survive but without Reverend Father
1817 Return to the Grande Chartreuse
1831–63 Reverend Father Dom Jean-Baptiste Mortaize: young candidates (363, 19th c)
1839 2-year novitiate followed by Solemn Profession
1851 1-year novitiate, 4 years in simple vows, followed by Solemn Profession
10 houses restored in France, 9 in Italy, 1 in Switzerland, 3 in Spain, 1 in Slovenia
New foundations in England and Germany

20th Century
1903 Expulsion from France – the Grande Chartreuse to Farneta (Lucca) Italy

1924   *Statuta Ordininis Cart.* (following the new Code of
        Canon Law)
1940   Return to the Grande Chartreuse (4 Charter-
        houses, one of nuns, already reinstated)
1949   2-year novitiate, 3 years in simple vows, Solemn
        Profession
        19 houses of monks, 5 houses of nuns
1969   2-year novitiate, 3 years in simple vows, 2 additional
        years of simple vows living with the solemn pro-
        fessed, then Solemn Profession
        (19 houses of monks, 5 houses of nuns)
1971 and 1975 *Renewed Statutes* (after Vatican II)

3

Vocation

**To the praise of the glory of God, Christ, the Father's
Word, has through the Holy Spirit, from the beginning
chosen certain men, whom he willed to lead into solitude and unite to himself in intimate love.** (Statutes
0. 1. 1)

A vocation is an extremely mysterious reality. The call of
God is not something extrinsic; it penetrates to the most
intimate centre of the heart. We are what we are on account
of this call.

To understand this reality a little better, let us first of all
listen to the Bible. We are immediately struck by the collection of great vocations it describes,[1] which are magnificently
recounted to us. They teach us much about the psychology
of those people who have been called and the way in which
God has seized them and continues to draw them in order
to reveal to them the vocation of which they are the object.

But if we step back a little, we are able to perceive that,
taken as a whole, the Bible is the history of one vocation,
the vocation of the people of God. It is from the womb[2] of
this common vocation enfolding everyone that the particular
vocation takes its meaning.

DEVELOPMENT OF THE IDEA OF VOCATION IN THE BIBLE

We need to study the way in which God has worked out this vocation over the course of centuries and how the people of God became progressively aware of it: little by little, by the pressure of events, they began to understand the depth to which their call had been rooted in them. They learned to describe it more and more precisely and accurately. This helps us the better to discern what God is saying: to renew for ourselves the discovery of the truth as he himself has planned it. The way by which God has guided his people from glory to glory remains for us an unerring path for penetrating the mystery of our own vocation.

THE OLD COVENANT

THE VOCATION OF ISRAEL

Israel is called into existence through the sign by which Abraham is chosen and consecrated to his mission. Through the innumerable accidents of their history, the people descended* from Abraham came to know itself as the people chosen by God. However obscure it may have been at the beginning, they knew that they were engaged in an absolutely unique relationship with God, that they were the recipients of a mysterious divine preference. It is this relationship that makes them aware of their true identity and constitutes them as a people.

It is above all the memory of the great events during Moses' time that marks this people and gives them their personality: the exodus from Egypt, the covenant of Sinai and the giving of the law, the wilderness, the conquest of the promised land.

The prophet Ezekiel later describes Israel's entry into relationship with its God through a striking image:

> 'I passed by you, and saw you flailing about in your blood. As you lay in your blood, I said to you, "Live! and grow up like a plant of the field." You grew up and became tall and arrived at full womanhood; your breasts were formed, and your hair had grown; yet you were naked and bare.
>
> 'I passed by you again and looked on you; you were at the age for love. I spread the edge of my cloak over you, and covered your nakedness: I pledged myself to you and entered into a covenant with you, says the Lord God, and you became mine. Then I bathed you with water and washed off the blood from you, and anointed you with oil.' (Ezekiel 16:6–9)

For a long time this was the notion around which the people expressed their vocation. God had 'found', 'encountered', 'called', 'chosen,' 'preferred' them. The words seem to suggest that the people pre-existed in the choice of God. At least, there is no sense of the need to dig more deeply.

After the Exile everything was different. There was a violent dislocation. Dislocation of people and land: the small remnant was wrenched from its land, found itself lost among nations of strangers, deprived of its temple, yet at the same time knowing that it was not deprived of its God (Ezekiel 11:16). God also was dissociated from the land. There was a greater consciousness of universalism, of the transcendence and uniqueness of God. Idols are reduced to nothing, to less than nothing. The Lord is the God of the entire universe, the almighty creator.

The people pondered the mystery of their vocation ever more deeply. Until the Exile, the possession of the promised land had seemed an integral part of the covenant. The sense of vocation and the theology of creation had to become deepened and reciprocal.

Let us pay close attention to this deepening. Something analogous must happen in us. The initial understanding that we have of our personal vocation is always more or less superficial and selfish. It is only after the destruction of our 'idols' and our 'ideals' by Providence, or by some other means, that we begin to touch the depth of our heart where the Word calls us to be . . . out of nothing.

TOLEDOT

Towards the middle of the period of the Exile, God raised up from among the people an extremely powerful and deep thinker who introduced a magnificent synthesis of the overall divine plan. We do not know his name. He was certainly a priest, so we call his work, the Priestly Codex, by the initial 'P'. This work formed part of the tradition that provided the framework for the redaction of the Pentateuch and thus conferred definitive meaning on all the historical details.

Through a series of narratives beginning with the Hebrew word *Toledot*: 'These are the generations (a history) of . . .' (Genesis 5:1; 6:9 etc.), 'P' linked the universal creation with the covenant of Abraham and the birth of the people, the entire history of Moses, and the Exodus and Sinai. Thus he made the plan of God visible, the whole natural order directed towards the divine, and the whole of the creation of the world directed towards the vocation of Israel. The author has fastened the first link of the generational chain to the very origin of things. The last link is the Gospel which is revealed to us in the book of the descent of Jesus Christ, son of David, son of Abraham (Matthew 1:1), son of Noah, son of Adam, son of God (Luke 3:23–38).

SECOND ISAIAH

Another great genius appeared at the end of the Exile, one who was completely different, who communicates the same doctrine to us in a more accessible form. A poet, a lyrical poet, he translated it into marvellously beautiful songs. Again, we do not know his name. He was a prophet who continued the lineage of Isaiah, and is called Second Isaiah. His work has been given the title, 'The Book of Consolation' (Isaiah 40—55).

Here again we find Israel's vocation very clearly and insistently bound to, and even identified with, its creation, and that in the perspective of the universal creation.

> But now thus says the Lord, he who created you, O Jacob, he who formed you, O Israel: Do not fear, for I have redeemed you; I have called you by name, you are mine. (Isaiah 43:1)

> . . . everyone who is called by my name, whom I created for my glory, whom I formed and made. (Isaiah 43:7)

THE WORD

This attachment of the notion of vocation to that of creation, which throws light on the all-powerful and absolute initiative of God, took place thanks to the deepening of the notion of the Word. 'P' has already shown us the world created solely by the Word of God (cf. 'God said' of Genesis 1). Second Isaiah mines this vein deeply: he sees creation as a call to existence. This intimation is only found with metaphysical precision in the Book of Wisdom ('How can anything exist unless you call it?' 11:25), but a form of it is constantly present in the Book of Consolation.

> Listen to me, O Jacob, and Israel, whom I called: I am

He; I am the first, and I am the last. My hand laid the
foundation of the earth, and my right hand spread out
the heavens: when I summon them, they stand at attention. (Isaiah 48:12–13)

The Word first manifests itself as creative: it calls, and
beings are; this is creation. It then reveals itself by assigning
to each its task. It calls these beings whom it has created;
this is the meaning of the vocation of each one. This Word
who in former times and in many ways addressed itself to
the people through the law and the prophets finally comes
in the image and likeness of a man to call each of us by our
name (Hebrews 1:1).

Thus the entire Bible, from the creation to the Incarnation,
may be seen as a manifestation of the divine Word. Second
Isaiah is its prophet, St John its evangelist.[3] The Word of
God calls every being into existence, each 'according to its
kind' (Genesis 1:11). Each being is made for something: the
tree bears within itself its own seed, but it does not need to
be told so; it is inscribed in the necessity of its nature.

Human beings, too, are made for something, and as we
are intelligent and free, God communicates his designs† to
us through his Word. 'God blessed them, and God said
to them, "Be fruitful and multiply, and fill the earth and
subdue it" ' (Genesis 1:28). And this in general is our
vocation, the source of all our inventiveness, of all activity.

But each person is also destined for a personal life of
knowledge and love of God. A friendship between two people
is always unique, and it is for this reason that an unspecified
call to existence and to activity is inadequate. There must
be a personal call, and this is to speak of vocation in its
proper sense, though still in a general way.

But there is an even more specific meaning: God destines
certain beings to belong to him in a particular way, through
consecration or for a mission. In the same way that the entire

people were consecrated, set apart for their God and charged with a particular mission, so the call addresses itself to certain people whose vocation the Bible describes to us. God needs, God deigns to need human beings. He guides his people through individuals, he admonishes, he teaches, he chastises, he delivers them by means of human beings. The great vocation of Israel crystallises, becomes particular, in diverse vocations: patriarchs, leaders, kings, judges, prophets, people of the Word, consecrated individuals, priests.

It is the wrong question to ask why God has called this person or that: he has made him for this. But one day, the one who is chosen hears the call. At the same time the discovery is made by those called – they know more or less obscurely that this is why they were created: for the pure service of God; and under this form, this revelation bears the grace needed to accomplish it.

In a certain way, vocation is already inscribed in our being – not as a necessity, not in the way that an apple tree bears apples and can only bear apples – but because everything depends on the free design† of God, of the unique Word who has called us to be in the light of this vocation, who has prepared us for it in the course of our life through ways that are frequently very mysterious, and who at last calls us to its fulfilment in the heart* of his Kingdom.

THE NEW COVENANT

The Word is made flesh in the womb* of the Virgin Mary. The Word of God is welcomed with such utter responsiveness that it is able to become flesh. In Mary's 'yes' is contained potentially the 'yes' of the Church and of all the saints. Human beings are on earth to say this 'yes', above all people of prayer, that is to say, people fully conscious of their humanity.

Henceforth, it is through his incarnate Word that God calls us to him. With this authority, Jesus calls the first disciples to follow him: 'Follow me.' After his return to the Father, it is ordinarily through the Spirit and the Church that his Word reaches us across the centuries.

The inalienable dignity of human beings is to be made in the image of God (Genesis 1:26–7) in all their being, in their intelligence, their liberty and love. But this liberty is fragile and the image of God is obscured by sin; the image attains its consummate revelation in the appearance of Christ. 'Behold, the man!' It is Christ who is willed by God to be the firstborn. Human beings have been created as a rough sketch of Christ. Only Christ can reveal us to ourselves. Only Christ is able to show us the Father.

> He is the image of the invisible God, the firstborn of all creation; for in him all things in heaven and on earth were created . . . through him and for him. (Colossians 1:15–16)

Human beings only attain the fullness of their humanity, are fully human, in their conformity to Christ through the activity of his Spirit, which implies for sinners a transformation so radical that it is a new creation through which as image they come to resemble the incarnate Word (1 Corinthians 15:49).

> Be renewed in the spirit of your minds, and clothe yourselves with the new self, created according to the likeness of God in true righteousness and holiness. (Ephesians 4:23–4)

> For those whom he foreknew he also predestined to be conformed to the image of his Son, in order that he might be the firstborn within a large family. (Romans 8:29)

How can this be?

And all of us, with unveiled faces, seeing the glory of the Lord as though reflected in a mirror, are being transformed into the same image from one degree of glory to another; for this comes from the Lord, the Spirit. (2 Corinthians 3:18)

The Christian is not a separate species of human being, but what each person ought to be. And the monk is not a separate species of Christian. He tries to be what each Christian ought to be. Conformity to Christ in faith, hope and love: this is holiness, and each person is called to this holiness.

But human beings do not exist in isolation. Humanity is one, the Body of Christ is one. It is animated by the unique Spirit who gives to each a personal place and function in the Church. As in the Old Testament certain people are called to play a particular role for the benefit of all.

But each of us was given grace according to the measure of Christ's gift . . . for building up the body of Christ, until all of us come to the unity of the faith and of the knowledge of the Son of God, to maturity, to the measure of the full stature of Christ . . . in love. (Ephesians 4:7, 12–13, 16)

We are going to try to deepen our vocation[4] in the light of the fundamental gifts of our faith. But let us quickly add that only love can justify the gift of all our being and all our life. This love has its inexhaustible source in the Father; its human face and its way in the Son; its strength in the Spirit; its end in the unity of all in the eternal communion of the blessed Trinity.

'Burning with divine love,
we made a vow.'
(Bruno)

4

The Call

The idea of vocation implies a call on the part of God and a response to that call on the part of the person. In the practical world, this is realised in many ways. At the same time, there are certain constants that we can consider.

THE ABSOLUTE INITIATIVE OF GOD

Before being an idea that comes from us, our vocation is God's idea, a choice: 'You did not choose me but I chose you' (John 15:16). This choice precedes even the existence of the person who is called: 'Before I formed you in the womb I knew you, and before you were born I consecrated you' (Jeremiah 1:5). It is the effect of an eternal decree in a moment of time: 'Just as [God] chose us in Christ before the foundation of the world to be holy and blameless before him in love . . . to the praise of his glorious grace . . . ' (Ephesians 1:4, 6).

This is the first link in the chain of events in our life.

> For those whom he foreknew he also predestined to be conformed to the image of his Son, in order that he might be the firstborn within a large family. And those whom he predestined he also called; and those whom he called he also justified; and those whom he justified he also glorified. (Romans 8:29–30)

We know that Paul used the past tense in this passage in

order to express his certainty that the movement initiated by God will reach its end while respecting our liberty.

At its source, the call is lost in the divine eternity. The word 'call' (*vocare*) evokes for us God's interpellation, or challenge, of a person already constituted as such. But it is clear that the Word of God touches us at an infinitely deeper level. As soon as it addresses us, it constitutes us as persons, calling each of us from nothing into being. Before this creative Word there is nothing, absolutely nothing. We are, because God calls us into existence. We are persons because God intimately addresses us with a personal Word.

To come before God at this ultimate level – there is nothing more, neither attainments nor misery, neither beauty nor ugliness, that has the power to attract the divine choice to us. It is uniquely in the being of God that we find the source, uniquely in this Subsistent Good that pours itself out by virtue of its own goodness.

> I have loved you with an everlasting love;
> therefore I have continued my faithfulness to you.
> (Jeremiah 31:3)[1]

'God is' means 'God loves'. Because God is love (1 John 4:8). It is not by an act that is other than his being, as it is for us, but by an eternal act that is none other than his being, all of his being. The source of our call is Love. 'Jesus, looking at [the rich young man] loved him and said . . . "Come, follow me" ' (Mark 10:21). The fact that God is love does not entail that he must love us through an inherent necessity. The liberty of God is absolute. Nothing constrains it. If God loves, it is because he wants to love. Love has no why. The love of God for his creatures is always a bridge thrown across an abyss. We cannot lay hold of Love. Each one of us can only receive with humble gratitude, full of wonderment. Is that not why we retain that exclamation so characteristic of

St Bruno: '*O Bonitas!*'? 'In this is love, not that we loved God but that he loved us ... We love because he first loved us' (1 John 4:10 and 19).

Israel, too, is aware of this gratuitous gift.

> It was not because you were more numerous than any other people that the Lord set his heart on you and chose you – for you were the fewest of all peoples. It was because the Lord loved you and kept the oath that he swore to your ancestors, that the Lord has brought you out with a mighty hand, and redeemed you from the house of slavery. (Deuteronomy 7:7–8)

St Paul warns us against all temptation to pride.

> Consider your own call, brothers and sisters: ... God chose what is foolish in the world to shame the wise; God chose what is weak in the world to shame the strong; God chose what is low and despised in the world, things that are not, to reduce to nothing things that are, so that no one might boast in the presence of God ... 'Let the one who boasts, boast in the Lord.' (1 Corinthians 1:26–9 and 31 (in part))

GOD'S SEDUCTION

> Therefore, I will now allure her,
>   and bring her into the wilderness,
>   and speak tenderly to her.
>   (Hosea 2:14)

Love seeks and effects a personal, intimate communion. Having decided to give us the gift of his love, of himself, God must nevertheless respect our freedom. Our love can only be free. The Lord will not compel us. He woos us, he leads us on 'with cords of human kindness, with bands of love' (Hosea 11:4).

He unveils some of his beauty through his creatures, above all, in Christ. He arouses in our hearts immense and deep aspirations that we can scarcely name. He makes us aware of our poverty, our sin, of our inner solitude. We can become afraid in the face of the unknown, or of the demands of Christ, which we know only too well: we can flee him, we can hide, but one day we must say 'yes' or 'no' to his call, to the offering of his love.

If we say 'yes', it is due to the deep attraction that God exercises over our heart, an attraction all the stronger because we are unable to say why.[2] Made in God's image, human beings are irresistibly drawn towards the Creator. We need to adore. We can but desire Goodness and love Love. We are made for light and union. In every time, in every place, people experience the attraction of God, and I will risk saying that each person adores him, even if sometimes they call him anti-God, or by some other name. Contemplatives of every religion are only people having a more acute sense of the divine, whom God calls to be more directly occupied with himself. These are our brothers and sisters.

Even so, the One who attracts us is not seen. 'But what is it that I love when I love God?'[3] exclaimed St Augustine. Like Augustine, the person who is drawn has great difficulty in saying. Perhaps it is just this that is an element of the attraction: 'Deep calls to deep' (Psalm 42:7). The time-lag between the real attraction that the beginner experiences and the expression that they are able to give it is well known and sometimes poses delicate problems of discernment. But it is certain that for a vocation to solitude and prayer there must be a profound sense of God, of his infinite mystery in which the solitary disappears by the unknown paths of the desert. We can get to the unknown only by unknown paths. God alone can lead to God. 'Alone' – this little word weighs on the monk (*monos*) as both an unbearable doom and a promise without limit that demands a complete integration of his being in love and truth. This solitude has no meaning, exists in truth only as the expression and the means to satisfy a thirst for intimate communion which is itself a response to the enticement of love. Lovers seek solitude in order to discover each other and become one. Love alone suffices. Only Love suffices.

A scribe asked Jesus,

> 'Which commandment is the first of all?' Jesus answered, 'The first is, "Hear, O Israel: The Lord our God, the Lord is one; you shall love the Lord your God with all your heart, and with all your soul, and with all your mind, and with all your strength." The second is this, "You shall love your neighbor as yourself." There is no other commandment greater than these.' (Mark 12:28–31)

THE STRUGGLE WITH GOD

Mary's serene and utter 'yes' is the expression of her simplicity and her purity of heart. More often God's call addresses itself to a complex heart, one that is divided and more or less wounded, that bears the scars of its sins and an often tangled personal history. This is above all true in our time. God's wooing encounters the resistance of the 'flesh' and becomes a scorching fire.

The one who is called contests with God. Sometimes we seem to be beaten, pursued by the Lord.[4] We know the importance of the theme of Jacob's struggle with God (Genesis 32:23–33) in monastic tradition. This struggle between the darkness and the light can last for years. Some-

times the person is marked in their body, like Jacob, who
from that time forward was lame.

Sometimes, too, this is an indication of a special mission
to be undertaken, which manifestly transcends the powers
of the one who is called. Thus the Lord as master calls
someone and leads them, like Peter, where they do not want
to go (John 21:18). Moses sought to hide from his mission
(Exodus 3 and 4). Paul said he was 'seized by Christ'
(Philippians 3:12). It is only after much suffering that he
understands that his weakness is the strength of Christ in
him: 'My power is made perfect in weakness' (2 Corinthians
12:7–10). How difficult it is to understand this, and to live
it in truth!

For Jeremiah, the struggle with God in his life was acutely
painful. It was unquestionably an extreme case, but such
extreme cases precisely throw into relief something that is
more or less intrinsic to many vocations that are somewhat
special.

> O Lord, you have enticed me,
>   and I was enticed;
> you have overpowered me,
>   and you have prevailed.
> I have become a laughingstock all day long;
>   everyone mocks me . . .
> If I say, 'I will not mention him,
>   or speak any more in his name,'
> then within me there is something
>   like a burning fire
>   shut up in my bones;
> I am weary with holding it in,
>   and I cannot.
>   (Jeremiah 20:7, 9)

The relationship is entirely unequal. Jeremiah would like to rid himself of his vocation, but the word has been implanted within him and, like an interior fire, consumes him. Note that this text is a monologue, like all the texts, called his Confessions, where Jeremiah shows us his affliction.[5] God does not answer, does not explain. Jeremiah feels abandoned by God. He does not understand.

How did this man whose vocation raised so many problems for him, which did violence to his vivid sensitivity, how did he manage to follow this way to the end, assuming in an apparently superhuman obedience a state that shattered him? This is a secret even from Jeremiah. Why did God drag his faithful messenger's life through such a terrifying night? This remains God's secret. Jeremiah's path is lost in wretchedness and this without any dramatic effect – lost like water in the sand. A man participates in the suffering of God before the sin of his people. The only freedom that seems left to him is the freedom to suffer.

We are so far from these attitudes, a little too clever and conscious of our 'rights', a stance that we sometimes risk adopting before God, forgetting that he is the Lord. In addition, the true face of our freedom is very mysterious. Are we sure we know what it is? We must place our freedom at the deepest level of our being, beyond all our interior and exterior conditioning, beyond the restlessness of our sensibility. Even the Jeremiahs, who are in fact exceptions, remain free at the root of their will to say 'yes' or 'no'.

And we must understand those who have been tested. The freedom of Jeremiah's words that sometimes verge on blasphemy does not in any way contradict the free and profound submission of his will. In his case, the opposite is true. Even Jeremiah's revolt is proof of his great love of God.

RESPECT FOR OUR FREEDOM

It is very important to distinguish divine 'constraint', which leaves our deepest freedom intact, and the sort of constraint that is psychological, interior or exterior, which diminishes or completely banishes it (Statutes 1. 9. 3).

Doubtless all sorts of social, economic, intellectual and other influences affect us. Doubtless each of us comprises a tangle of factors coming from our heredity, our childhood, our personal history. Doubtless our sins, our refusal to love, have weakened and blinded us. Doubtless our motives are more complex and less unselfish[6] than might first appear. The human heart is deep.

In the meantime, none of this constitutes an insurmountable obstacle for God's action. He takes us as we are. It is sometimes precisely by means of our limitations and our wounds that he can lead us to himself. A psychological evaluation of our personality and our life, however accurate and exhaustive, is relevant only at the level of the psychological mechanisms in question. A more complete and human reading of these traits is equally possible, one that takes into account our inalienable and creative freedom, and, even more complete and infinitely more profound, one that is spiritual. It is here that a very delicate discernment of spirits comes into play.

A clear-eyed and utterly sincere effort is indispensable. Nonetheless, let us be assured that our true liberty is our 'yes', in view of which God has given us being and existence. It is exercised in its fullness to the extent that we respond to our vocation. It can never be in contradiction with the call that God has made from all eternity and in time. On the contrary, it is in allowing ourselves to be led and formed by the Spirit, according to the will of God, that we become free with the true liberty of the children of God for which Christ has set us free. 'Now the Lord is the Spirit, and where the Spirit of the Lord is, there is freedom' (2 Corinthians 3:17).

It is the strength of Love and the light of the truth of Christ that little by little allows us to claim the inheritance of our freedom. 'If you continue in my word, you are truly my disciples; and you will know the truth, and the truth will make you free' (John 8:31–2).

5

Sell Everything That You Have

THE RICH YOUNG MAN

The story of the rich young man (Mark 10:17–22; Matthew 19:16–22; Luke 18:18–23) is particularly significant for us. One day in the third century, a young Egyptian named Anthony heard this reading at church: 'Jesus said to him, "If you wish to be perfect, go, sell your possessions, and give the money to the poor, and you will have treasure in heaven; then come, follow me" ' (Matthew 19:21). He understood these words of Christ to be addressed directly to him. Without hesitating, he put them into practice. He sold his possessions and retired into solitude. Anthony was to become the father of Christian hermit life.

The Word of God is living and penetrates like a sword. The Spirit wields it in the heart of those who listen. In this way it often happened among the first monks that they received a word of Scripture in such a way that it seemed as if a Word of God addressed them in the here and now, and they translated it simply and severely into their lived reality.

But in the gospel account, the man does not rise to the word. Why? Let us follow the narrative, so rich in spiritual teaching. Mark's account contains valuable concrete details. It specifies that 'a man ran up and knelt before him' (Mark 10:17). This is a man full of enthusiasm and fervour. And his intention is right. He wants to know the way 'to inherit eternal life'. Christ's response is rather chilling. The young man's enthusiasm is perhaps too human.

' "No one is good but God alone" ' (Mark 10:18). All created good is but a reflection of the divine good and must be referred to it. God has revealed his will in his law. 'If you wish to enter into life, keep the commandments' (Matthew 19:17). And Christ cites the ten commandments.

The young man responds with complete candour. ' "I have kept all these; what do I still lack?" ' (Matthew 19:20). He is fervent, certain of his righteousness. And yet something bothers him. He lacks something. But what?

There are two answers to this question, both to be found in the Gospels. According to Mark and Luke it is not enough to observe the prohibitions of the Decalogue; we also have to love our neighbours positively and to share with them our riches. The apocryphal Gospel of the Hebrews glosses the early narrative, adding these reflections: 'And the Lord said: "How do you say, I observe the law and the prophets? For it is written in the law: you shall love your neighbour as yourself [Leviticus 19:18]: and here are many of your brothers, sons of Abraham, clad in filth, dying of hunger while your house is full of possessions, and absolutely nothing goes out of it to them . . ." '

Thus the first answer is that his was a case of lack of awareness, a superficial self-satisfaction. The young man's observance of the law was too negative: he did not kill, did not steal, etc. He kept himself from doing evil but he did not love positively enough or effectively. 'For the whole law is summed up in a single commandment, "You shall love your neighbor as yourself" ' (Galatians 5:14), even to the point of renouncing your possessions. Note that the Lord did not mistake the undoubted good will of the young man. 'Jesus, looking at him, loved him' (Mark 10:21). It was through love that he opened his eyes and showed him the way of life: ' "You lack only one thing; go, sell what you own, and give the money to the poor, and you will have treasure in heaven; then come, follow me." '

Matthew cites the precept of brotherly love (Leviticus 19:18) among those the young man said he had observed (Matthew 19:19). As a result, the gift of his possessions to the poor is not considered as a concrete expression of the commandment to love your neighbour. It becomes a form of 'perfection' that transcends the commandment of Leviticus 19:18, which is put on the same plane as the negative prescriptions of the Decalogue, and it too becomes a way of transcendence: the gift of his possessions to the poor.

IF YOU WOULD BE PERFECT

Matthew begins Jesus' second response with these words: 'If you wish to be perfect'. The perfection in question is that of the new law brought by Christ, the law of love. This perfection is demanded of every Christian, because all are called in the Sermon on the Mount to be perfect as our Father in heaven is perfect (Matthew 5:48 – the only other verse in which the word *teleios* is used in Matthew).

By this single action, the young man is invited to go beyond the exact observance of the old law to the more radical demand of the Gospel. He has made good use of his possessions. He has fulfilled the law. He even senses that there is something else that must be offered; but he does not know what it is. It is everything. 'Go, sell your possessions, and give the money to the poor.'

In essence, it is not a question of the amount of the sacrifice, it is a completely other way that Christ proposes to him, that of poverty, a complete stripping, for the freedom of love. The perfection of love is the complete gift.

It is not a question of distinguishing two states of Christian life: that of simple Christians who content themselves with observing the prescriptions of the law (vv. 18–19) and that of the 'perfect' (v. 21) who give all that they have to the poor. The word of the Lord, while leaving everything to the freedom of the person called – if you like – nevertheless is pointing out the only true way to eternal life (see Matthew 6:19–21; Luke 12:33).

'When the young man heard this word, he went away very sad, for he had many possessions.' Even the gaze of love which Christ fixed on him was unable to elicit a response. Why? He is ensnared in his possessions. They are the chains that enslave him, that deprive him of freedom of spirit. We may also surmise that the wealth of the rich young man consisted not only in material possessions, but also his virtue, his good conscience. He went away, sad, torn between the love of Christ and the love of riches, that is to say, in the last analysis, the love of himself. Sadness is frequently linked to wealth, to love of self. Joy is the patrimony of those who become poor for God. We may be reminded of the joyful way in which Francis of Assisi addresses Lady Poverty.

HAPPY ARE THE POOR

There is in all this something that is difficult for some people to accept: that sinners and prostitutes precede the 'righteous' (the scribes, the Pharisees, the rich young man – serious people) into the kingdom of heaven (Matthew 21:31).[1]

Is sin, then, the indispensable condition for receiving the Gospel? Does practical fidelity to the law close the door to Christ? Certainly not. The evidence is in Christ's first disciples, who for the most part had been through the demanding school of asceticism and prayer of John the Baptist. After they had lived faithfully in this way, Jesus presents them with an invitation to climb higher. But here they part company. The apostles can say, 'We have left everything and followed you' (Matthew 19:27). Others, like the young man, go away discouraged.

In both cases there has been moral preparation. In the one case, they are ready to go on. On the other, they have settled down, content with themselves, 'in the right' with God. But a life that has congealed is dead. The trap is even more formidable in that the righteousness of life is genuine and acquired by altogether praiseworthy effort. The mistake is to claim the virtue, to attribute it to oneself. In this case, one is aware of innocence; one is not aware of weakness. Even more, an irreproachable life runs the risk of developing tightly involuted self-love and tenacious spiritual pride. One is secure in oneself, and this easily results in severity towards others. By the same token, when a big sacrifice is required, such a person is unable to make it.

Only humility and a radical poverty can elude the snare. A lively awareness that everything is a gift of God. An obstinate refusal to appropriate anything at all to oneself. A readiness that is always open to follow the Lord.

The one who is more aware of being sinful and weak, once he has turned towards God, is sometimes more responsive. He has less baggage. Inversely, his being is wounded and weak. But the most important thing in the spiritual life is not our integrity but that grace is able to work in us.

> Then Jesus said to his disciples, 'Truly I tell you, it will be hard for a rich person to enter the kingdom of heaven. Again I tell you, it is easier for a camel to go through the eye of a needle than for someone who is rich to enter the kingdom of God.' When the disciples heard this, they were greatly astounded and said [and we with them], 'Then who can be saved?' [Let us listen well to the response because it contains all of our hope.] But Jesus looked at them and said, 'For mortals it is impossible, but for God all things are possible.' (Matthew 19:23–6)

COMPLETE RENUNCIATION

The doorway to life is poverty of spirit, of heart, in the biblical sense. This law always obtains. Abraham, the first to be called, had to leave his country, had to be ready to offer Isaac in sacrifice. The people of God had to pass through a process of progressive deprivation in the desert before entering the land of Promise (Statutes 1. 4. 1).

The gentle Christ demands sacrifice, not of this or that, but of everything, absolutely everything.

> Whoever loves father or mother more than me is not worthy of me; and whoever loves son or daughter more than me is not worthy of me; and whoever does not take up the cross and follow me is not worthy of me. Those who find their life will lose it, and those who lose their life for my sake will find it. (Matthew 10:37–9)

The human response must be without reserve and immediate.

> As they were going along the road, someone said to him, 'I will follow you wherever you go.' And Jesus said to him, 'Foxes have holes, and birds of the air have nests, but the Son of Man has nowhere to lay his head.' To another he said, 'Follow me.' But he said, 'Lord, first let me go and bury my father.' But Jesus said to him, 'Let the dead bury their own dead; but as for you, go and proclaim the kingdom of God.' Another said, 'I will follow you, Lord; but let me first say farewell to those at my home.' Jesus said to him, 'No one who puts a hand to the plow and looks back is fit for the kingdom of God.' (Luke 9:57–62)

If one is not committed to going the whole way, it is better not to begin.

'Whoever comes to me and does not hate father and mother, wife and children, brothers and sisters, yes, and even life itself, cannot be my disciple . . . For which of you, intending to build a tower, does not first sit down and estimate the cost, to see whether he has enough to complete it? Otherwise, when he has laid a foundation and is not able to finish, all who see it will begin to ridicule him, saying, "This fellow began to build and was not able to finish" . . . So therefore, none of you can become my disciple if you do not give up all your possessions.' (Luke 14:26–8, 33)

One whole dimension of the monastic life is the expression of this radical renunciation. (See Statutes 1. 10. 6 on profession; ch. 3. 28 on poverty; ch. 1. 7 on ascesis, etc.)

IF HE DIES

Why this radical demand? Christ teaches us a way to life. Why, then, this sharp paring, this hewing of the body? To renounce all sin, all that colludes with sin in our fallen and feeble state – this is easily understood. To free our heart for love – 'Where your treasure is . . . ' (Luke 12:34) – this goes a long way. But the Gospel seems to go even further: you must hate your own life, lose it, in a word, die. And this is bound up with the death of Christ.

Jesus answered them, 'The hour has come for the Son of Man to be glorified. Very truly, I tell you, unless a grain of wheat falls into the earth and dies, it remains just a single grain; but if it dies, it bears much fruit. Those who love their life lose it, and those who hate their life in this world will keep it for eternal life. Whoever serves me must follow me, and where I am, there will my servant be also. Whoever serves me, the Father will honor.' (John 12:23–6)

St Paul lived this in eminent fashion. He can clarify for us:

> I regard everything as loss because of the surpassing value of knowing Christ Jesus my Lord. For his sake I have suffered the loss of all things, and I regard them as rubbish, in order that I may gain Christ and be found in him . . . I want to know Christ and the power of his resurrection and the sharing of his sufferings by becoming like him in his death, if somehow I may attain the resurrection from the dead. (Philippians 3:8–9a, 10–11)

Thus it is a matter of death in Christ in order to live in Christ: 'I live, but it is not I who live, but Christ in me' (Galatians 2:20). Death gives rise to transfiguration, a passage to a higher life. Death is the law of life. It is the paschal mystery realised in us.

This is a Christian truth that can be applied to all without exception. The monk seeks the realisation of this death within himself, in the present, in this world, in order to have eternal life in God in this life. His grace is radical. To see the Truth in its full transparency; to offer ourselves utterly in an act of love in which all our being is involved; or go beyond the fragmented character and impotence of all our acts – these are the aspirations that flow from the image of God inscribed in our being. Death is profoundly bound up with love.

The life of the monk is perhaps rightly considered to be an anticipation of death, or rather of the life that is born from death in Christ, that is to say, in and through love. This death, while being a brutal tearing away at the sensible level (this is the wages of sin), is freedom from all the claims that hold us in slavery, above all the chain of the disordered love of self. This death seeks to be transparency to truth, enlarging of our being to cosmic dimensions, new birth in Christ.

This freedom does not reach its fullness until the moment of our death.[2]

WITH GOD, EVERYTHING IS POSSIBLE

In the contemplative life this renunciation must be effected in our inmost heart. Only pure hearts may see God (Matthew 5:8). The more intimate the union to which we aspire, the greater our purity of heart must be. Only simple and humble poverty is able to receive the Infinite without appropriating it. Only pure love, that seeks no return for itself, can love Love.

It is good to be aware from the beginning that it is this to which we are called: not to a perfection or usefulness according to our standard, but an almost unbearable, shattering encounter with Love that ravages and burns all that is not him.[3]

This prospect can disconcert and discourage us. If we rely only on our own resources, we have reason to be discouraged. This is what normally happens to those beginners who set out to strip the 'self' with great enthusiasm. They do not notice that they are only feeding the self and their pride with their effort, as St John of the Cross remarks so harshly: 'All the good works of beginners are worth nothing, or almost nothing.'

But, for all of that, the beginner should not be discouraged. No human being is able to accomplish this work. Only God is able to purify the human heart and to give us love in truth. Little by little, seeing our good will, he takes the task in hand, without our even knowing how, and brings it to a good end. After all, it is completely natural for us to live in deep poverty. We are, in truth, just this poor. If only one day we come to love truly, even if only a little, or even a very little, it is worth while.

This is indeed the secret. All the hard language of stripping is only the negative aspect of the language of love. For one who loves, the focusing of all their heart on the beloved is taken for granted and this does not require continual efforts of the will. *Amor meus, pondus meum*, said St Augustine. Love, by the gravity of attraction, draws all our being towards the beloved. It is in this way that the burden of Christ is light, because the love of God has been poured into our hearts through the Holy Spirit (Romans 5:5). Rather than becoming absorbed in disengaging ourselves from our chains, one by one, let us focus our attention and our heart on the Lord, asking him unceasingly for the gift of love. The rest will follow, by the grace of God.

> When the disciples heard this, they were greatly astounded and said, 'Then who can be saved?' But Jesus looked at them and said, 'For mortals it is impossible, but for God all things are possible.' (Matthew 19:25–6)

6

Follow Me

Clearly this theme evokes the Exodus during which Israel travelled through the desert, following the Lord who guided her by the pillar of cloud and fire (Exodus 13:21). For us it is a question of following Christ. It is not enough to strip ourselves of everything. A being empty of love for creatures quite simply is a being without love. We must bind ourselves to Christ.

He says to us: 'Follow me', I who am 'the Way, the Truth and the Life'. All the rest proceeds from this personal love for Christ: to keep the commandments, to hear his teaching, to live and die like him, to love as he loves.

The disciples of Jewish rabbis in Jesus' time were not formed simply by book learning. They lived with their teacher, they watched him translate his doctrine into the many and various circumstances of life, in order to understand it through these living principles.

Thus Jesus' actions were not unfamiliar. Only, Jesus was never an official accredited rabbi – he did not study at a school of recognised teachers. He appeared as an itinerant teacher – 'rough', 'lay', we might say, or perhaps, 'charismatic' – whose sole authority was his own person and the truth of his teaching. He had not yet performed any miracles when he called his first disciples. To attach themselves to him signified for them to share his life and destiny – an uncertain destiny, but one which awakened in them their deepest hopes. These hopes were disappointed, at least materially, that is to say, in an immediate and political sense: 'We had hoped that he was the one to redeem Israel' (Luke

24:21). Thus these hopes were in part an illusion; they had not yet been raised to the true perspective of the Kingdom, and as if blindly, without knowing where they were led, they decided to follow him.

Jesus announces the Kingdom of God. It is the hour of judgement and of salvation. The call is urgent. Those who hear him in a specific way must follow him unconditionally. For those who want to become involved with Jesus and with whom Jesus involves himself, it is all or nothing. Following Jesus demands all of our being, all of our existence.

Notice that it is Jesus who decides when it is a question of following him full time – he can also refuse (Luke 8:38). He assumes responsibility for the destiny of those whom he receives as disciples.

Let us therefore follow Christ with his first disciples. Let us pay attention to his teaching, because no one ever spoke as he did. His words are eternal life (John 6:68). Let us contemplate his way of being: poor, chaste, free from all sin, gentle and humble of heart; but courageous and just, not favouring anyone when the truth needed to be spoken, not seeking glory from men, but uniquely concerned with doing the will of his Father, towards whom he constantly turns his gaze; welcoming children, the sick, the poor; with infinite mercy towards sinners – forgiving as his Father in heaven forgives – seeking them out, breaking all barriers and conventions; capable, sometimes, of a holy anger; hard towards the self-satisfied pride and the hypocrisy of the Pharisees; but loving people no one else has ever loved; even his enemies he loved to the end; he bound his disciples with bonds of love that also assured the cohesion of their small group (it is by love that they can be recognised as his); he is uniquely concerned for the Reign of God, the things of his Father, above all the shabby trivialities of human beings. He entrusted himself in full confidence to the providence of the

Father; he was entirely given to his mission without counting the cost and without any self-seeking.

His disciples saw him drive out demons, usher in the Reign of God through the power of his miracles. They began to perceive something of the mystery of his person. They followed him enthusiastically along the roads of Palestine. Victory was in reach. Then the end of his preaching, mortal opposition by religious authorities, Jersualem, betrayal, the Cross, death. And the disciples? Those who were formed by his own hand, so to speak? Those who vowed with Peter to go with him to death rather than deny him (Matthew 26:35)? 'Then all the disciples deserted him and fled' (Matthew 26:56).[1]

There is something cruel in the way that this last phrase reiterates almost word for word the narrative of the initial scenes of vocation. 'They left everything and followed him' (Luke 5:11). In St Luke's account, after the arrest, those who accompanied Jesus are not called 'disciples' (*mathētai*); later they are called by another name (the Eleven and their companions), and in the Acts of the Apostles, the expression *mathētai* belongs to the Church.

The disruption of the disciples at the moment of the Passion is of decisive importance. Between Christ and his first disciples yawns the unbridgeable abyss of the Cross. There the disciples cannot follow. The end of the earthly way of Jesus is the Cross; it is his specific vocation. He alone can submit to it, solitary, bearing the burden of all. The idea of following Jesus is not to be understood as if it were a question of imitating a great man such as we might take as a model for our own life, a Gandhi, a Socrates, for example; Christ and his disciples are not on the same plane. The Cross is unique. Even if the believer of today has in some way the possibility of walking the road that took Jesus to the Cross and resurrection it is still uniquely thanks to the grace of the One risen and glorified. It is only after Easter that the disciples are able to follow Jesus to the end, because following Christ reveals itself as being much more profound than a simple invitation of an ethical order, or something merely exterior.

PAUL

St Paul, for example, who was not around at the time of Jesus – save, perhaps, as an enemy – does not describe any of his life as following in Jesus' footsteps. For him, this distinctive form of existence, which is the privilege of those who lived close to Jesus, is a privilege not possible after Easter. Paul locates the believer in the heart of the paschal mystery so as to live by it. Once he has asserted this essential distance that faith establishes between the Lord and his disciple, Paul plunges the believer into an incredible closeness to the Lord, whose life and sufferings we share (Colossians 1:24). We are crucified with Christ (Galatians 2:19; 6:14) so as to participate by anticipation, sacramentally in baptism and existentially in the new Christian existence, in the hoped-for resurrection (Philippians 3:10–21; Ephesians 2:6). Love has been poured into our hearts (Romans 5:5), through faith and baptism we become a single being, a single mind with him; it is Christ who lives in us. It is a profound mystical union, but without confusion. The closeness itself creates the distance. The more intimate the union with Christ to which the Christian is invited, the more it is seen as nothing other than an inconceivable grace. Even a participation in Christ's saving passion cannot proceed from an insufficiency in the fullness of suffering which the historical Christ took upon himself;[2] it can only come from an incomprehensible grace by which we are allowed to take part in this fullness.

Christian holiness in the course of history is nothing other than the unfolding of the grace of Christ, the vitality of the

Spirit of Christ that animates the Church and its saints. This explains why it is sometimes one aspect of the life of Christ, sometimes another that comes to light in the saints and in the permanent institutions of the Church, in which diverse charisms are incarnated. Otherwise, each Christian ought materially and fully to reproduce the whole life of Christ.

Following Vatican II, 'Let religious see well to it that the Church truly show forth Christ through them with ever-increasing clarity to believers and unbelievers alike – Christ in contemplation on the mountain, or proclaiming the kingdom of God to the multitudes, or healing the sick and maimed and converting sinners to a good life . . . always in obedience to the will of the Father who sent him' (*Lumen Gentium*, 46). Let us add: in the temptation in the desert, in his love even unto death and his intercession with the Father, and it will not be difficult to discern the forms of Christ's love for his Father and for human beings that we are called to live.

JOHN

St John can help us to deepen our own specific vocation, because John dares to bridge the insuperable gulf caused, in the Synoptics, by the disciples' running away and, in St Paul, by faith. He lives so utterly in the love of the Lord that he knows himself to be in the place to which the Lord has transported him over the abyss of the Cross. In the Synoptics too, the women remain at a distance and gaze on the cruci-fixion. What these women foreshadow becomes in Mary, the mother of Jesus, a full reality: follow Christ even to absolute destitution, such utter helplessness that we have to be aban-doned to it even by the Son: 'Behold your Son'. John, who is to give shelter to the destitute mother, represents the Church, awakening from the sleep of the solitude of the

Cross, and coming forth from the open heart, from which is poured the ultimate gift of blood and water that symbolise the sacraments and the Spirit. Because the sacraments spring from this place, the Cross, and because the disciples who now have fled were in communion before the Passion, they are, whether they want it or not, members of the unique body of Christ, at the foot of the Cross and on the Cross.

There, with the profound penetration of these events by the light of Easter that characterises him, John, instead of showing the disciples fleeing, has Christ dispersing them himself: 'Let these men go' (John 18:8). The same applies to the promise made to Peter who would follow him to the end: 'Where I am going, you cannot follow me now; but you will follow afterward' (John 13:36). In effect, John reveals that, beyond their flight, there is the possibility of being near Jesus through faith and love in contemplation of the Word made flesh.

John also passes over in silence the cry of dereliction in the night of the immolated Christ. For him, the love that moves everything is so visible that there is never any doubt about its identity. It is precisely when it reaches 'the end' (John 13:1) that it shines most clearly as love, and that it causes faith to give birth to redeemed humanity's response, in Mary and John. It is a kind of contemporaneity between the time of Christ and that of the Church.

In virtue of the grace that radiates from the exalted Christ – both on the Cross and in glory – the Church, Marian and contemplative, follows Jesus even across the gulf created by the Cross, which meanwhile remains (John 13:36; 16:18–20; 17:11). As this following after Jesus is essentially realised for John in the loving surrender of faith, the difference between the first generation and those that followed is very much blurred for him. The life of the first disciples who followed Jesus becomes a sort of archetype for all the later disciples, whose faith, too, can be a following of Jesus because, according to John, the *response* of the first disciples was already a response in faith.

From John we rejoin the spiritual tradition (for example, Ignatius of Loyola and his 'Spiritual Exercises') in which that following of Christ essentially signifies being at the disposal and call of Christ and following after him, through all the episodes of his life up to the Cross, but also up to the resurrection.

In his beatitude, John unites those who cannot 'see', who only believe, with 'those who see' (20:29). He extends his hand to those who come after and passes on 'what we have seen with our eyes, what we have looked at and touched with our hands, concerning the word of life' (1 John 1:1), in this way establishing 'the fellowship . . . with the Father and with his son Jesus Christ' (v. 3). In his prophecy, Jesus foretells persecutions for the Church (John 15:18—16:4), and brings to light the common destiny which binds to the Lord those who believe and love. 'The servant is not greater than the master' (John 15:20). Note that such conformity does not negate the distance between Christ and the disciple. He ever remains the Lord and Master (13:14), the unique King (18:37). No one can stand before the throne of the Father except the Lamb that was slain (Revelation 5:6). Nowhere is it indicated that the disciple should seek out or provoke persecution and suffering for the sake of a greater conformity to the Lord.

Perhaps Ignatius of Loyola touches the main point when he thinks that the highest disposition of the disciple, notwithstanding the desire to be conformed by grace to the Lord even in suffering, consists in leaving to God alone the free choice of distributing the truly christological graces of suffering (*Exercises* 98, 147, 167). This 'indifference' that places the will of God higher than any individual programme of perfection is essential for an authentic conformity to Christ.

In short, John shows us that at the point where love and

faith converge in contemplating, on the one hand, the incarnate Word, and on the other, the mystery of Christ made present in the sacraments, the sacrifice of the Mass and the gift of the Spirit, there time and space are transcended, and we are able to commune with Mary and John in the life and death of the Lord, in a sense that is mystical but very real. In this way we can plunge into the flood of redemptive love that flows uniquely from the Cross, and by grace become that love as well.

We will return to the thought of St John in the next conference. To finish today, I would like to help you see to what point the idea and the reality of following Jesus impress their sign on all of Carthusian life.

FOLLOWING CHRIST IN THE STATUTES

It is Christ who through the Holy Spirit has chosen us and led us into solitude to unite us with himself in intimate love (Statutes 0. 1. 1).

The goal of our life is expounded to the candidate as being 'the glory that we hope will be given to God by our sharing in the work of Redemption, and how good and joyous it is to leave all things and hold fast to Christ'. If the candidate is not shaken by the austerity of our life and 'readily promises, on account of the words of the Lord, to walk this difficult path, desiring to die with Christ and to live with Christ', he is accepted (2. 17. 7).

Guigo presents Christ as the model *par excellence* that the Carthusian ought 'above all to imitate . . . This same Lord and Saviour of mankind deigned to live as the first exemplar of our Carthusian life, when he retired alone to the desert and gave himself to prayer and the interior life; treating his body hard with fasting, vigils and other penances; and

conquering the devil and his temptations with spiritual arms'
(0. 2. 10).

In the same way, the novice is ineluctably confronted with
temptations 'which are wont to beset the followers of Christ
in the desert' (1. 8. 16). For our young monks, 'we follow
Christ in his fast in the desert' (1. 7. 1). We accept the
trials and afflictions of our life, 'embracing poverty with the
freedom of God's sons, and by renouncing our own will'
(1. 7. 1), after the example of Christ who suffered for us in
order to give us this example to follow (1. 7. 1).

Everything in our life bears the imprint of Christ. Even
sickness and age conform us ever more perfectly to Christ,
if they are accepted in trusting confidence (3. 27. 1).

All of the ascetical life is to be viewed from this angle,
since 'mortification of the flesh' arises in the first place from
our promise to follow Christ's call before all else. We should
practise it 'primarily to be freed from the tendencies of our
lower nature and enabled to follow the Lord more readily
and cheerfully' (1. 7. 3). And then, there is something very
significant. We do not give an absolute value to penances.
They are the means used for an end: following Christ. Thus
the Statutes continue,

> But if, in a particular case, or with the passage of time,
> someone finds that any of the aforesaid observances is
> beyond his strength, and that he is hindered rather than
> helped in the following of Christ, let him in filial spirit
> arrange some suitable measure of relaxation with the
> Prior, at least for a time. But, ever mindful of Christ who
> calls, let him see what he can do; and what he is unable
> to give to God by common observance, let him offer in
> some other way, denying himself and taking up his cross
> daily. (1. 7. 3)

Novices 'learn to chasten by the spirit the misdeeds of the
flesh, and to carry in the body the death of Jesus so that

the life of Jesus may also be manifested in their bodies'
(1. 7. 4). And again,

> By penance, moreover, we have our part in the saving
> work of Christ, who redeemed the human race from the
> oppressive bondage of sin, above all by pouring forth
> prayer to the Father, and by offering himself to Him in
> sacrifice. Thus it comes about that we, too, even though
> we abstain from exterior activity, exercise nevertheless an
> apostolate of a very high order. (4. 34. 4)

'For the solitude of the cell is the place where a soul,
enamoured of silence, and forgetful of human cares, becomes
a sharer in the fullness of the mystery by which Christ crucified, rising from the dead, returns to the bosom of the Father'
(6. 41. 4). All of the hidden life of the cell is a single following
of 'Jesus in the hidden and humble life of Nazareth, either
praying to the Father in secret, or obediently laboring in his
presence . . . our activity, therefore, springs always from a
source within us, after the manner of Christ, who at all times
worked with the Father in such a way that the Father dwelt
in him and himself did the works' (1. 5. 7).

'Both brothers and fathers, by conforming themselves to
him who did not come to be served but to serve, manifest
in different ways the riches of a life totally dedicated to
God in solitude' (2. 11. 5).

The profession of vows of poverty, obedience and chastity
is regarded as a way of following Christ. 'The monk has
elected to follow Christ in his poverty and by this poverty to
be enriched' (3. 28. 1). At the time of his profession, the
monk disposes of all his possessions in order to follow Christ
(1. 10. 6).

Obedience is 'a spirit of voluntary submission, so that in
solitude they may more fully conform themselves to the
obedient Christ' (3. 23. 9). 'Following the example of Jesus
Christ, who came to do the will of his Father, and who

taking the form of a servant, learned obedience through what
he suffered, the monk subjects himself by Profession to the
Prior, as God's representative, and thus strives to attain to
the measure of the stature of the fullness of Christ' (1. 10. 13).

Chastity is the response of hearts who want to be undiv-
ided, 'who have been taken possession of by Christ'
(2. 13. 14). Its fruit is a 'solitude [where] the monk's soul
[is] like a tranquil lake, whose waters well up from the purest
sources of the spirit and, untroubled by news coming from
outside, like a clear mirror reflect one image only, that of
Christ' (2. 13. 15).

The secret of solitude is that it is the place where 'is ever
being enacted the great mystery of Christ and his Church'
in all its depth, in a way that is pre-eminently realised in the
Virgin Mary (0. 2. 1; 1. 10. 1).

The Novice Master 'will be solicitous that the love of his
charges for Christ and the Church grows daily' (1. 9. 4). Our
part is, like Mary of Bethany, to be seated at the feet of the
Lord to listen to his word (1. 3. 9). 'If life with Christ and
intimate union of the soul with God were lacking, faithfulness to ceremonies and regular observance would be of little
profit, and our life could be justly compared to a body
without a soul' (1. 9. 5).

It is only in union with Christ that the offering of the
monk's life becomes acceptable to God. 'On the appointed
day, the future professed makes his vows after the Gospel or
the *Credo* of the conventual Mass (5. 36. 13–14); for then, the
offering of himself, which he intends to unite to that of
Christ, is accepted by God through the hands of the Prior'
(who celebrates the Mass) (1. 10. 8).

Priestly consecration is a profound configuration to Christ-
priest: 'After the example of Christ, the monk likewise
becomes both a priest and a sacrifice whose fragrance is
pleasing to God; and through this association in the Lord's

sacrifice, he shares in the unsearchable riches of his Heart'
(1. 3. 8).

The community is constituted a 'Carthusian church'
through and in the sacrifice of Christ.

> All this finds its source and support in the celebration of
> the Eucharistic Sacrifice, which is the efficacious sign
> of unity. It is also the centre and high point of our life,
> as well as being the spiritual food for our Exodus in
> solitude, by which through Christ we return to the
> Father. Throughout the entire Liturgical cycle, Christ
> prays, both for us as our Priest, and in us as our Head;
> hence it is that we may hear our voices in him and his
> voice in us. (1. 3. 7)

We are to be 'true disciples of Christ, not merely in name
but in deed; let them be zealous for mutual love, living in
harmony, forbearing one another, and, if one has a complaint
against another, forgiving each other' (1. 3. 4).

Finally, 'For to this alone do these Statutes tend, that,
guided by the Gospel, we may walk in the way of God and
learn the breadth of love' (4. 35. 1).

FOLLOWING CHRIST IN VATICAN II[3]

> In the Constitution which begins, 'the Light of the
> World', this most sacred Synod has already pointed out
> how the teaching and example of the Divine Master laid
> the foundation for a pursuit of perfect charity through the
> evangelical counsels, and how such a pursuit serves as a
> blazing emblem of the heavenly kingdom . . .

> From the very infancy of the Church, there have
> existed men and women who strove to follow Christ more
> freely and imitate Him more nearly by the practice of the

evangelical counsels. Each in his own way, these souls have led a life dedicated to God. Under the influence of the Holy Spirit, many of them pursued a solitary life, or founded religious families to which the Church willingly gave the welcome and approval of her authority.

And so it happened by divine plan that a wonderful variety of religious communities grew up. This variety contributed mightily toward making the Church experienced in every good deed (cf. 2 Timothy 3:17) and ready for a ministry of service in building up Christ's body (cf. Ephesians 4:12). Not only this, but adorned by the various gifts of her children, the Church became radiant like a bride made beautiful for her spouse (cf. Apocalypse 21:2); and through her God's manifold wisdom could reveal itself (cf. Ephesians 3:10).

But whatever the diversity of their spiritual endowments, all who are called by God to practise the evangelical counsels, and who do so faithfully, devote themselves in a special way to the Lord. They imitate Christ the virgin and the poor man (cf. Matthew 8:20; Luke 9:58), who, by an obedience which carried him even to death on a cross (cf. Philippians 2:8), redeemed men and made them holy. As a consequence, impelled by a love which the Holy Spirit has poured into their hearts (cf. Romans 5:5), these Christians spend themselves ever increasingly for Christ and for His body the Church (cf. Colossians 1:24).

Hence the more ardently they unite themselves to Christ through a self-surrender involving their entire lives, the more vigorous becomes the life of the Church and the more abundantly her apostolate bears fruit.

. . . Since the fundamental norm of the religious life is a following of Christ as proposed by the Gospel, such is to be regarded by all communities as their supreme law.

7

You Will See

John the contemplative reveals to us some intimate aspects of the call of Jesus and the role of the disciple. The basic text is the account of the call of the first disciples, John 1:35–51:

> The next day John again was standing with two of his disciples, and as he watched Jesus walk by, he exclaimed, 'Look, here is the Lamb of God!' The two disciples heard him say this, and they followed Jesus. When Jesus turned and saw them following, he said to them, 'What are you looking for?' They said to him, 'Rabbi' (which translated means Teacher), 'where are you staying?' He said to them, 'Come and see.' They came and saw where he was staying and they remained with him that day. It was about four o'clock in the afternoon. (John 1:35–39)

THE TESTIMONY OF JOHN THE BAPTIST

It is the testimony of John the Baptist that attracts the attention of the two disciples to Jesus. In the same way, the following day, Andrew introduces his brother, Simon Peter, to Jesus, then Philip introduces Nathanael. The calls multiply like a kind of contagion, making use of familial and political relationships, etc. Sometimes God calls directly (Abraham, Paul). More often, we hear his voice through mediation, intermediaries between God and us: people, events, reading. Samuel did not understand that the Lord was calling him until the priest Eli discerned the presence of God in the mysterious call: ' "Go, lie down; and if he calls you, you shall say, 'Speak, Lord, for your servant is listening' " ' (1 Samuel 3:9). ' "It is the Lord" ' (1 Samuel 3:18).

In his turn, Samuel called David to be king of Israel and anointed him. All the prophets are bearers of God's word and responsible for making his will known. But God also avails himself of people who are unaware of their role, without even specifically believing in him, for example, Cyrus (Isaiah 45:4–5).

Each Gospel, but St John's especially, is the testimony of people who have seen to those who have not seen, so that they may believe. In a very real way, each of us receives our faith and the intuition of our vocation in particular, thanks to other people, through created intermediaries. This economy is not left at the threshold of the monastery. We receive the legacy of a tradition. We are always in need of a guide and the support of a brother or father.

WHAT DO YOU SEEK?

This is the first word that Jesus speaks in the Gospel of John. It is the first question that Christ addresses to those who want to follow him.

The Prior asks the candidate who is to receive the habit, 'What do you seek?' We know the word of St Bernard, *'Ad quid venisti?'* It is a question we should continue to ask throughout our lives.

The Statutes are very clear. When a candidate presents himself to become a monk, he is asked about his motives and intentions. There is one criterion: that he truly seeks God alone (Statutes 1. 8. 6). How? In dying with Christ in order to live with him (Statutes 1. 8. 7).

Every other consideration becomes secondary: birth,

social background, intelligence, etc., all that concerns the
candidate's person; or for that matter, all that concerns his
intention: the opportunity to study, human development,
health, a search for exotic experiences, dissatisfaction with
the modern world or the Church as it is, misanthropy, natural
taste for solitude, renunciation, peace, and even prayer.

Over the long term only the search for God is able to give
meaning to our life and create a balanced person. It is
because they are, consciously or unconsciously, seeking
something else that dissatisfied people who seem to have
failed to reach psychological or affective integration are to
be found in monasteries. Frequently they are engaging in
displacement behaviour in some slightly marginal activity:
studies, an office, the 'reform' of the house or the Order,
etc.

The disciples in the Gospel were already searching. They
had been in the school of John the Baptist. He was only a
man but he pointed them to the true light. So too in our
day, many people have their interior desire awakened before
they have a clear knowledge of Christ. Frequently they are
baptised but not practising; the Church they know does not
speak to them clearly enough about what they are groping
for. Sometimes they find the light in philosophy, in beauty,
in natural sciences or esoteric teaching, in Oriental religions,
Buddhism, etc., and all this serves to lead them to Christ by
revealing something of the mystery of God. John shows us
that the origin of this search is to be found in the Father.
'All those that the Father gives me will come to me' (6:37).
And again, 'No one can come to me unless it is granted by
the Father' (6:65).

This way does not always come to fruition. The multi-
plicity of doctrines, attachment to sin or a subtle pride can
veil the face of Christ. Christ is able to speak to 'Jews' who
in John's stylistic scheme are the type of anti-disciples: 'You
will search for me, but you will not find me; and where I

am, you cannot come' (7:34). They refuse to recognise in
Jesus the Son of God. They are blind.

The decision to allow to prevail the love that comes to us
from Jesus is identical to the vision of this love that comes
through the believing response to love. The opposite decision
makes a person blind to the light that comes and such a
person remains in the darkness of unbelief and the absence
of love (1:5; 3:19; 12:35).

Here is our terrible power: we can open to the radiance
of love to be enabled to love, or we can close ourselves in
the hell of a heart that does not want to love. To find Jesus,
we must follow him, we must live with him, with all that
implies of love and deep rooting in him. Jesus is the only
and absolute revelation of love, and only this love itself is
able to see him.

There is a grand unity in St John. He seems to contemplate
a unique reality, which he presents through different perspectives, that we can never perfectly recover. I will content
myself with presenting a survey of three aspects of following
Christ: 1) the Johannine vision; 2) the analogy of Jesus–Father: disciple–Jesus; 3) the figure of the disciple whom Jesus
loves.

1. COME AND YOU WILL SEE

HUMAN VISION

Let us reflect for a moment on human vision. First, let us
note that in its optical evolution the eye is designed for light:
it does not perceive objects but the light reflecting from
objects. The object is visible only because light renders it
luminous. What we see is light united with the object, a sort
of marriage, in which light takes the object's form and makes
it visible. This is how light makes things available.

When it is a question of people, exterior light is not enough. By itself, it cannot make us present to another except as an object. We can close up, put on a mask, which almost always is indicative of a more or less conscious attitude of escape or denial. To be present as a person, to agree to be seen as a subject, we must make a free gift of ourselves to the gaze of the other. This gift is an offer of personal communication which in the final analysis is love, based on an act of trust in the other. The light should radiate from within.

On the part of the one who looks on, it is important to point out that human vision is more than a function of sense and physiology. It can perceive in sensible things spiritual relationships and unite them by embracing them. It is able to do this above all in the presence of the visible and audible signals of people who are expressing themselves freely, and to whose call it reacts positively or negatively. All the richness of intuition and human sensibility come into play in a gaze that sees the heart of the other in their facial expression. To be perfect, this gaze requires an extremely flexible openness, a certain quality of attention, a profound respect before the mystery of the other, and above all a responsiveness to the truth of their being, which is expressed in welcoming the other exactly as they are. This gaze is also a humble offering of love and trust. On the part of the other, it is possible to refuse. It is only when both offers of love and trust meet that people see each other in truth.

In human vision, the whole person is involved. Because of this we understand that our capacity for welcoming the other is precisely conditioned by our capacity to welcome God. 'Those who do not love a brother or sister whom they have seen, cannot love God whom they have not seen' (1 John 4:20). Because only the pure hearts will see God (Matthew 5:8).

TO SEE GOD

To see God, 'the eyes within the eyes', according to Isaiah (52:8)[1] is the deepest desire of the old covenant. The nostalgia for paradise which dominates the whole Bible is first of all the awareness of having lost direct and familiar contact with God. Fallen humanity cannot see God and live. The Lord is a hidden God, and his wrath is to be feared. And yet human beings seek his face unceasingly (Psalm 24:6), and know that there is no happiness apart from this vision. The prayer of Moses on Mt Sinai is typical: ' "Let me see your glory" ' (Exodus 33:18), as is the Lord's response: ' "I will shield you with my hand as I pass by – you shall see my back. You cannot see my face" ' (Exodus 33:23). It is only in Christ's Incarnation that God offers himself to human gaze in the supreme gift of his love. Listen to the awe in John's testimony:

> We declare to you what was from the beginning, what we have heard, what we have seen with our eyes, what we have looked at and touched with our hands, concerning the word of life . . . we declare to you what we have seen and heard so that you also may have fellowship with us; and truly our fellowship is with the Father and with his Son Jesus Christ. (1 John 1:1, 3)

The Word of Life, life eternal, is made visible, audible, near, tangible. It is by this sensible means that God reveals himself to humanity, that his divine life is communicated. It is by this sensible means that human beings receive and welcome him.

However, if sensible perception is the point of departure for spiritual perception and communion with God, it contains a more exalted reality, one that penetrates and transfigures it, one that requires it to go beyond itself in a radical purification.

THE DEGREES OF 'SEEING'

The person of Jesus constitutes the centre of the vision. Everything rests on 'seeing Jesus' in the reality of historical time. But this 'seeing' includes various stages: simple visual perception, attentive and searching observation, contemplation, deep penetration of the object, and communion with him.

All Jesus' contemporaries saw him: the disciples, the crowds, the Jews. Everyone saw his signs. Twice during his Passion, Pilate presented him to the crowd. 'Behold the man' (19:5). The soldiers gazed on 'the one whom they had pierced' (19:37). The Johannine paschal testimony is essentially summed up in this formula: 'We have seen the Lord' (20:18 and 25).

In each case, the 'seeing' is effectively at a different level, and goes from without to within. At the lowest level there is an opacity to what is seen, a non-seeing: these are the Galileans who, in spite of the signs performed before their eyes, are not able to see that Jesus himself is the true bread (6:36 and 40). There is the non-seeing of the Pharisees who say: 'We see' (9:41). There is the world that refuses to see (15:24).

Even the disciples' eyes are not fully open before the Passion (14:7–9). It is the 'hour' of Jesus that enables them to see, the hour in which the Son of Man is glorified (John 12:23; 17:1). It sheds a decisive light on all of his life.

In its fullness, Johannine 'seeing' penetrates beneath the exterior surface of appearances to the fundamental level of being, to the source of light that it contains, to the secret of inmost life.

THE OBJECT OF 'SEEING'

The object of Johannine contemplation is in the first place the glory of Christ. 'And the Word became flesh and lived among us, and we have seen his glory, the glory as of a father's only son, full of grace and truth' (1:14). This glory is a mysterious and paradoxical reality; it is the ineffable divinity of God in its free manifestation.[2]

The glory has shone out and the disciples have contemplated it in the flesh of Jesus, in a completely real and concrete human being, in all the congenital weakness of humanity, given up to death. It was the glory of the only Son, which he derived from the Father and thus reveals the Father. ' "Who has seen me has seen the Father" ' (14:9). Here is the ultimate object of Johannine 'seeing': the Father.

All of John's work is a pedagogy of spiritual 'seeing', pointing towards the 'icon' of the Father, that is, the humanity of his incarnate Son, resplendent in the glory of the 'hour' (13:31–2). The 'seeing' is not the consequence of a deduction from faith, proceeding from the divine dimension perceived in Jesus. It is a question, rather, of true seeing. 'See the Father' does not mean a secondary instance of seeing and does not imply a secondary visual image beyond (or 'behind') the person of Jesus which must be penetrated in order to reach the Father. It is in Jesus that the Father is perceived. The glory of the Father radiates in the glory of the Son. The disciple who opens his eyes on the person of Jesus in his human condition, his flesh, opens his eyes to the mystery, and sees truly, however indirectly, the Father. This must not be understood in either an unstable or a static sense. It is in the boundless obedience of the Son that the boundless love of the Father, and thus his very being, appears.

Here we touch the heart of Christian contemplation in its irreducibility and specificity, because it is earthed in the absolute newness of the mystery of the Incarnation, the union of the human and the divine, the flesh and the spirit.

I WILL MANIFEST MYSELF TO HIM

John's insistence on the concrete nature of 'seeing' appears to pose a problem. We are among those who 'have not seen and who have believed' (20:29); are we called to live a not-seeing faith?

Certainly the immediate and sensible presence of Christ in historical reality as lived by privileged witnesses undergirds the structure of faith. However, this perspective is incomplete until the paschal mystery has retrospectively illuminated it. While Jesus lived on earth, the disciples had difficulty 'seeing' him, that is to say, understanding his true personality and recognising his unique relationship with the Father. ' "Have I been with you all this time, Philip, and you still do not know me?" ' (14:9). But at the time of the revelation of his glory through the Cross and resurrection – 'again a little while' – a new era is ushered in. 'In a little while the world will no longer see me, but you will see me;[3] because I live, you also will live. On that day you will know that I am in my Father, and you in me, and I in you' (14:19–20).

The world will be unable to perceive Jesus after his death (7:34; 8:21) because it never saw anything of him but the external and transitory aspects. The disciples saw him, and recognised that he was in the Father. They understood at last what was said by the person and the life of Jesus, but only when the last word of the sentence was spoken,[4] that is to say, the death and resurrection. The precondition for this understanding, truly to see Jesus, is an absence: they cannot see the one who returns to the Father (16:7), for a little while. This little while is as much the *Triduum Mortis* as, for the Church, the duration of the world in time.

Through a profound mystery of love, the absence of Jesus,

the absence of vision in the earthly sense, makes possible a more intimate form of presence[5] and of 'seeing'. The appearances are only the prelude to a more interior and universal manifestation of the mystery of Jesus through the Spirit to every disciple who believes and loves.

> 'They who have my commandments and keep them are those who love me; and those who love me will be loved by my Father, and I will love them and reveal myself to them . . . and we will come to them and make our home with them . . . The Holy Spirit, whom the Father will send in my name, will teach you everything.' (14:21, 23, 26)

TRANSFIGURING CONTEMPLATION

The interior presence of Jesus, the love of the Father and the activity of the Spirit create a deepening and a transformation that establish a contemplation that sees and does not see at the same time. Jesus was no longer seen directly as the first disciples had seen him, and certainly we cannot yet see him as on the last day. 'We know that when he appears we shall be like him for we shall see him as he is' (1 John 3:2).

Now is the time when we see him indirectly, conveyed by the account of the historical Jesus, and also through the life that is quickened in the Church by the Spirit. On a spiritual plane, the difference between those who have seen the Risen Christ and those who believe 'without having seen' is taken up in the beatitude ('blessed', 'happy') of intimate union with the Father, the Son and the Holy Spirit of those who 'see' in faith and love, and become in this way the divine reality that they contemplate. Contemplated Love transfigures us into that which it is.[6] 'From now on we are God's children' (1 John 3:2), from now on we are born of Love for love.

> And we have seen and do testify that the Father has sent his Son as the Savior of the world . . . So we have known and believe the love that God has for us. God is love, and those who abide in love abide in God, and God abides in them. Love has been perfected among us in this: that we may have boldness on the day of judgment, because as he is, so are we in this world. (1 John 4:14, 16, 17)

> Everyone who loves is born of God and knows God. Whoever does not love does not know God, for God is love. (1 John 4:7–8)

St John conceives the process of salvation in this way: in God, the essence of life is love, light is the radiance of this love; in us, the vision of the life which has been brought to us by the Incarnation of the Word reproduces in us the love that brought him to birth.

> 'I ask not only on behalf of these, but also on behalf of those who will believe in me through their word, that they may all be one. As you, Father, are in me and I am in you, may they also be in us, so that the world may believe that you have sent me.' (17:20–1)

The priestly prayer gives us a real glimpse that through union with Christ, the disciple in some way receives the seal of Trinitarian life. To which subject we now turn.

2. JESUS AND HIS DISCIPLE: THE FATHER AND JESUS

Jesus is the shepherd of the sheep. 'He calls his own sheep by name' (written 'on the white stone . . . a new name that no one knows except the one who receives it' (Revelation 2:17) – and even that one knows it only little by little) 'and he leads them out. When he has brought them all out he goes ahead of them and they follow because they know his voice' (10:3–4). The heart instinctively recognises the voice of Christ. 'I know my own and my own know me, just as the Father knows me and I know the Father' (10:14–15).

The rapport between Jesus and those who follow him is analogous to that between the Father and Jesus. Jesus, in his relationship with the Father, is thus the model for the disciple. 'Whoever says, "I abide in him," ought to walk just as he walked' (1 John 2:6).

How did Jesus live? In the most intimate union of love with the Father: a union of mutual knowledge (see John 10:14–15); a union of reciprocal presence: 'On that day you will know that I am in my Father, and you in me, and I in you' (14:20); 'So that they may be one, as we are one, I in them and you in me, that they may become completely one' (17:22–3); an absolute union of wills.

The disciple can do nothing apart from Jesus, just as Jesus can do nothing apart from the Father.

> 'The Son can do nothing on his own, but only what he sees the Father doing; for whatever the Father does, the Son does likewise.' (5:19)

> 'I am the vine, you are the branches. Those who abide in me and I in them bear much fruit, because apart from me you can do nothing.' (15:5)

As Jesus' food is 'to do the will of him who sent me and to complete his work' (4:34), so the love of the disciple is not real if it is not manifested in keeping the commandments. 'Now by this we may be sure that we know [=love] him, if we obey his commandments . . . whoever obeys his word, truly in this person the love of God has reached perfection.

By this we may be sure that we are in him' (1 John 2:3 and 5).

But the commandments of Jesus are summed up in the law of love (15:12–14). It is therefore in this love that the disciple is recognised (13:34–5), love that makes him worthy to be loved by Jesus (15:9–10).

Here we might cite the entire farewell discourse of the Last Supper. But let us content ourselves with this pericope of John 15:7–17, and let us allow the light from these words to penetrate our heart. Further commentary is not needed. (The upper-case letters on the left indicate the sections in the chiasmus.)

A   If you abide in me,
       and my words abide in you   PRAYER
       ask for whatever you wish,
       and it will be done for you.

B   My Father is glorified by this,
       that you bear much fruit   FRUIT
C   and become my disciples.

D   As the Father has loved me,
       so I have loved you;   LOVE
       abide in my love.
       If you keep my commandments,
       you will abide in my love,
       just as I have kept my Father's
          commandments
       and abide in his love.

E   I have said these things to you so
        that my joy may be in you,
       and that your joy may be complete.   JOY

D' This is my commandment,
    that you love one another   LOVE
    as I have loved you.
    No one has greater love than this,
    to lay down one's life for one's friends.
    You are my friends if you do what
        I command you.

    I have made known to you everything
    that I have heard from my Father.

C' You did not choose me
    but I chose you.
B' And I appointed you to go and bear fruit,
    fruit that will last,   FRUIT
A' so that the Father will give you
    whatever you ask him in my name.   PRAYER

    I am giving you these commands that you may love one
    another.

WHERE DO YOU LIVE?

Thus the disciple loved by Jesus is called to give his life
through love just as Jesus had given his (15:12–14;
10:17–18). If he follows him in the same way to make the
ultimate gift of his own life, he will have the privilege of
finally arriving at the place where Jesus is.

Where did Jesus live? 'Whoever serves me must follow me,
and where I am, there will my servant be also. Whoever
serves me, the Father will honor' (12:26).

And again: 'And if I go and prepare a place for you, I will
come again and will take you to myself, so that where I am,
there you may be also' (14:3).

In the priestly prayer: 'Father, I desire that those also,

whom you have given me, may be with me where I am, to see my glory, which you have given me because you loved me before the foundation of the world' (17:24).

To discover where Jesus lives is finally to arrive where he is, in his glory, the possession of which constitutes eternal life. Thus it is only then that the sentence that ends the story of the call of the first disciples discovers its full meaning. 'He said to them, "Come and see." They [the disciples] came and saw where he was staying, and they remained with him' (1:39).

In a very significant way, the analogy that exists in the relationship of coinherence between the disciples and Jesus and between Jesus and the Father also is verified here. The disciple 'whom Jesus loved' is 'on the breast' of Jesus at the Last Supper.

3. THE DISCIPLE WHOM JESUS LOVED

This mysterious figure[7] is the type of the disciple. We have seen the disciple defined in terms of love (15:8–10). The perfect disciple is the one who is loved by Jesus and excels in love. He has no other name than 'the disciple whom Jesus loved'. This name speaks his being. He is absent from the evangelist's account of the public life of Jesus. He appears for the first time at the Last Supper, as the one whom Jesus loves, at the very centre of the mystery of love and sacrifice. It is to him that Jesus reveals the sorrowful secret of Judas; he tells Peter. Much later, it is thanks to him that Peter was able to get into the court of the high priest (18:15–16). Alone of all the disciples he remains at the foot of the Cross in the moment of supreme darkness. He receives Mary as his mother and from that day onwards gives her a permanent home (19:25–7). Mary and the disciple visibly represent the Church that believes and loves. When Mary Magdalene brings news of the empty tomb, he runs there with Peter. He arrives at the tomb before Peter. Peter enters first and sees the linen wrappings; the beloved disciple follows and of him alone it is said, 'he saw and he believed' (20:8). The same quick intuition, the same instinct for love, are present in the scene of the appearance by the Sea of Tiberias after the resurrection. Jesus, on the shore, called the disciples who were in their boat. It is the 'disciple whom Jesus loved' who is the first to discover the identity of the Lord when they catch the fish, and says to Peter, 'It is the Lord!' (21:7). Jesus at last seems to promise him a particular destiny, distinct from that of Peter. 'If it is my will that he remain until I come, what is that to you?' he says to Peter. This enigmatic phrase seems to signify not only that the beloved disciple will continue to be present in the Church through the testimony that is preserved in the Gospel of John (19:35), but perhaps more profoundly, that this disciple represents the contemplative whom the Church will never lack.

The beloved disciple is characterised by love alone, and by the penetrating faith that bestows love, faith that enables him to reveal the Lord to the hierarchy of the Church (in the person of Peter). He is plunged deeply in the mystery of the Eucharist and the Cross. He is loved by Christ with a particular and personal love. In return, his heart seems absorbed in the person of Jesus. He believes, he sees. He remains until the coming of Christ. He receives the Mother of Jesus in his care – the Mother, who bears the whole Christ.

8

The YES in Time

The call of God is not something precise that sounds at a particular moment and exists entirely in the past. Certainly we become conscious of a call at a privileged moment of time, but the call itself is a creative word of God that springs from his eternity. The first moment in which we become aware of it never exhausts it. It continues to resonate throughout our life. It reveals its full meaning only as we come to understand our entire history. Our yes to this call therefore opens a story, a story whose outcome we cannot foresee in advance.

We must not think of a call as a reality that is predetermined in advance, programmed, a card that is punched by our initial yes that is then processed by a computer that relentlessly programmes the remainder of our life. Instead, we are asked in each moment, drawn by the Spirit, always to go forward a little further along an unknown way. We should always have the attitude of one who is called, who follows the Master at the new beginning of each day. Like the servant of the Lord:

> Morning by morning he wakens –
> wakens my ear
> to listen as those who are taught.
> The Lord God has opened my ear,
> and I was not rebellious,
> I did not turn backward.
>
> (Isaiah 50:4–5)

Our docility to the Spirit is inscribed in time as a dynamic faithfulness, a yes to God that is always open and responsive. Here, a problem arises. How can I commit (vows, etc.) a future that I do not know or control? Will not this very commitment hinder the action of the Spirit, retard the movement of our life?

The response to this question can only be found in God. It is he who has called us by a real commandment to be a complete gift. 'You shall love the Lord your God with all your heart . . . ' It is the Spirit that impels us. It is to the Lord that we are committing ourselves, even if we cannot know exactly what that will entail. Because of this, we can only abandon ourselves to God with complete trust, knowing that what he has begun he will bring to a good end.

GOD'S FIDELITY

It is, in the first place, God who commits himself to us. And he is faithful with an unshakeable fidelity that is the foundation of our fidelity. The Lord is our rock, our fortress, our shield. His faithfulness does not depend on ours. He cannot deny himself. He remains faithful even in the face of our faithlessness (Romans 3:3). 'God is faithful; by him you were called into the fellowship of his Son, Jesus Christ our Lord' (1 Corinthians 1:9). 'God is faithful and he will not let you be tested beyond your strength' (1 Corinthians 10:13).

In the Bible, God reveals himself as the living God who is and who will be with his people in their struggles, as the one who shows himself to be faithful to his promises and his covenant (see Deuteronomy 7:7–9). His fidelity is loving with irrevocable tenderness, love inexhaustible. Fidelity binds God's strength to human weakness in which, against all reason, he places his trust. God risks linking his name and his being with a fickle partner. That God is faithful characterises not his own ontological immutability, but his irrevocable choice in time (Isaiah 45:23). He shows his faithfulness through his action in history, through his commitment even to the extent of the Incarnation and the death of his Son. This faithfulness pours from him, eternally creative and ever new. Like his being, his faithfulness to us is a mystery, and the faces it reveals are ever a source of wonder. Sometimes it seems to move circuitously and to write straight with crooked lines.

From the human point of view, the person is subject to time in the sense that time is linear and progressive and is not complete. But the person prevails over time, is able to disengage from it and through thought to link past and future, and in this way to commit to the future. Human beings transcend the mere movement of becoming and give it meaning. A person's faithfulness gives coherence and meaning to a moment of time. Its truth is not necessarily in the spontaneity of the present instant, frozen exactly as it is, isolated, but in what proceeds from the choice and the engagement of deepest being: an engagement that triumphs over the parcelling out of time and that gives unity and coherence to each life. Such was the unfolding of Mary's *Fiat*; it matured in her like the Word himself through the long years of hidden and simple life in Nazareth, through her pondering of the often enigmatic events of the life of Jesus (the presentation in the temple, the three days that he stayed among the teachers there, Cana); through being entirely receptive to the growing illumination during her Son's public ministry; through her faithful presence at the foot of the Cross; through her place at the heart of the Church as it awaited the Spirit. It is only when the fruit is entirely ripened that the Lord places it next to him in his glory.

THE DAILY ROUND

It is not the moments of exaltation, the religious experiences, even dramatic ones, that can come to us, that are most important in our monastic life. What is most important is perseverance in daily prayer, the fidelity of each day in the way we have chosen, continual effort so that we live for the Lord, today, following the Spirit of his love the whole day through. Sometimes this continuity conceals a mystery of privation and poverty. It is hard to leave the fashioning to God in such a way that we renounce all self-determination, in any given moment, to remain simply before God for the unfolding of our life, for what has been and what remains to be. To persevere in a sort of open expectation, without anxiety, without forcing a conclusion. Nothing else. This can be an expression of the most personal bond with Christ, of a radical faith: we entrust him entirely with our being, so that he, uncontrolled and uncontrollable, may do with us what he wills. In consequence, this attitude renders us able always increasingly to abandon our own efforts to make our own mark in order to bear more deeply the mark of the Son's self-abandonment to the Father, and there to allow its redemptive virtue to penetrate humanity, the Love that is the life of the blessed Trinity.

THE TREE

Blessed are those who trust in the Lord,
    whose trust is the Lord.
They shall be like a tree planted by water,
    sending out its roots by the stream.
It shall not fear when heat comes,
    and its leaves shall stay green;

in the year of drought it is not anxious,
and it does not cease to bear fruit.
(Jeremiah 17:7–8)

First it is a seed that falls from a tree. It is small, a whirligig, spiralling through the air, carried by the wind's playfulness in a random dance along with other seeds. It is independent, free, giddy in the sunlight, full of promise, but changeable, a little irresponsible, we might say. In this way it travels far, sees a lot of things from outside, without engaging any of them. Then, one day, it must assume responsibility for the life it carries within itself. It finds a place, the place where it must grow. It buries itself alone in the dark earth. It disappears. It seems dead, but it is undergoing a transformation. It loses the shell that has protected it in its youth, and the heart of its substance becomes exposed, without light, vulnerable, but because of this, able to draw nourishment from the earth for its life. Little by little it adapts to its new mode of existence, it puts out roots towards the sources of life, it gathers strength from them, its being opens up, grows, and the light attracts it. It pushes a fragile shoot towards the sun, which gives it warmth. It is dressed with fresh and tender foliage. It is not alone. It sees other young trees, its brothers and sisters, growing around it. It breathes its joy in prayer. Its mouth is pressed against the earth to drink in its substance. Its arms open to the sky to welcome the rain, the warmth and light. It unites earth and heaven in a symbiosis of light. Its being is its prayer.

It holds firm in its place. It bends before the storm but springs back again. It is docile to the annual seasonal rhythm of death and life. It is stripped by winter winds and cracked by the cold, the frost. Its slender limbs are etched stark and black against the heavens. It endures the long sterility of winter, withdrawing its life within itself, waiting patiently.

When the earth wakes up, the sap rises in the tree. It puts

forth new leaves that shelter birds; its buds appear, develop, the flower blossoms, the fruit forms under the sun. It gives what it has received in all simplicity, to the good and the bad without distinction. It gives shelter to everything in its shade. When its fruits are ripe, the first to arrive can gather them. It does not keep anything for itself. Through the simple fact of its being, it softens the violence of the seasons; it strengthens the soil around it, preventing erosion. Its purest substance goes into the seeds that it makes and then launches on the adventure of life. It does not resist the onset of autumn. It adorns itself with gentle colours. Its dead leaves cover the ground in a sumptuous tapestry. Once again it enters the season of death, silently, with faith, a testimony to steadfastness through the flux of time.

9

The School of the Holy Spirit

THE HOLY SPIRIT IN OUR STATUTES

'The grace of the Lord Jesus Christ, the love of God, and the communion of the Holy Spirit be with all of you' (2 Corinthians 13:13).

The communion (*koinonia*, fellowship) of the Holy Spirit: intimacy, love, life with the Holy Spirit. Let us re-read the first paragraph of the Statutes, paying attention to the role of the Holy Spirit.

> To the praise of the glory of God, Christ, the Father's Word, has through the Holy Spirit, from the beginning chosen certain men, whom he willed to lead into solitude and unite to himself in intimate love. In obedience to such a call, Master Bruno and six companions entered the desert of Chartreuse in the year of our Lord 1084 and settled there; under the guidance of the Holy Spirit, they and their successors, learning from experience, gradually evolved a special form of hermit life, which was handed on to succeeding generations, not by the written word, but by example. (Statutes 0. 1. 1)

It is through the Holy Spirit that Christ chose men to lead into solitude and to unite with them in intimate love. It was by responding to 'this call', and therefore summoned by the Holy Spirit, that Bruno with his six companions entered the desert of Chartreuse. It was 'living in the school of the

Holy Spirit' and from experience that they developed our life.

Further on, the Statutes (Statutes 0. 2. 1) declare that it was the Spirit who 'entrusted the compilation of the first laws of our Order' to Guigo, the fifth prior of the Chartreuse.

In the Statutes we shall find 'both the form and the sacrament of that holiness to which each of us has been predestined by God', who are called to embrace this vocation. And yet, without the Spirit, they are nothing, because 'it is the Spirit who gives life, and he does not allow us to remain content with the mere letter' (Statutes 4. 35. 1).

Accordingly, 'it is not, indeed, enough to obey the commands of our superiors and observe faithfully the letter of the Statutes, unless, led by the Spirit, we savour the things of the Spirit.' (Statutes 4. 33. 2).

But the government of the monastery ought to be charismatic: 'The Prior . . . does not judge according to human standards, but together with his monks strives to listen to the Spirit in a common seeking of the will of God' (Statutes 3. 23. 8). 'He should not act as if good external order were his sole concern, but rather by his own docility to the Spirit he should mirror to all the love of Christ' (Statutes 3. 23. 19).

A CHARISMATIC VOCATION

These texts[1] make us aware of the charismatic nature of our vocation. The word 'charismatic' today tends to be associated with a particular movement called 'charismatic' and with religious manifestations that are a little spectacular. However, *charisma* is a Greek word for grace. It is applicable to all grace, to every gift of the Holy Spirit. In a more restricted sense, it refers to gifts given to particular people for the good of all. It is the breath of the Spirit that quickens the members of the Body of Christ, and gives birth to the

activities and states of life that express the vitality of the
Church and build it up.

Monasticism, with its origins in the fourth century,
appeared as an essentially charismatic movement. It
remained so for as long as it remained a living reality in the
West as it was in the East. It did not appear as an element
in the hierarchical structure of the Church but in the lineage
of holiness of life as a grace of the Holy Spirit, who impelled
people, laity for the most part, to realise the perfection of
Christian life in a new and radical way. This did not imply
opposition either in principle or fact to the hierarchy and its
existing structures at the time. On the contrary, bishops,
such as St Athanasius, encouraged the movement and sup-
ported it. Subsequently, the Church has always given monastic life its attention and consideration.

However, we may ask if this very fact and, in addition, the
cenobitic tendency which quickly prevailed, did not entail
an institutionalisation of monasticism that caused it to lose
something of its primitive and charismatic character, the
aspect that was creative and a bit anarchic. Theologians
have shown that there should not be opposition between the
hierarchical and structural dimension of the Church and its
charismatic dimension, when in fact, in the real world, there
is always a certain tension between them. This is not necessarily bad. Life is sustained by certain creative tensions.

Our Order is now a venerable institution with a long history, with massive buildings and practices. We risk forgetting
that all of this is nothing but a body without a soul if we are
not quickened by the breath of the Spirit of God. We risk
forgetting the precarious and audacious character of adventure of our first Fathers for whom entry into the Chartreuse
desert meant leaving behind them well-established and
honourable lives and careers to leap into the unknown
and into a very real poverty, without knowing how all of it
would end.

The risk and the spiritual unknown are real for us, too, but the venerable character and stability of institutions tend to hide them. We must never forget the desert's unpredictability, the complete despoliation that the desert requires, and the intimacy in which we alone, before God alone, may live in the depths of our soul. Our personal vocation cannot be reduced to a pre-established social reality, although it may be inserted into that reality. Each one of us must listen to the Spirit in his heart and follow his grace faithfully. For each of us, as for the Church, there can be a creative tension – though sometimes an unhappy one – between our grace, our personal charism, and our insertion into a pre-established tradition. Let us be convinced that it is the Spirit of Christ who is at work in the entire situation. The truth undoubtedly is to be found in a dynamic symbiosis between form and spirit, between the acquisitions of the past and the audacious impulse towards the future. Without this tension, there can be no life.

THE DIVINE MELODY

Christ is the way to the Father. We must follow him. We want to. But we are like people without any musical knowledge who hear a great classical symphony. We are moved. Unheard until now, its chords resonate in us. A yearning to create beauty takes hold of us. This is nothing but a passing fancy: we do not know how to do it because the laws of music are hidden from us. And even if we learn them, we discover that we are not musicians; we lack the sensitivity to the beauty of sound and the inspiration to communicate it that makes the musician.

Thus we are in the presence of the matchless melody that is Christ. 'Follow me,' he says, 'love as I have loved.' We want to so much, Lord. We have left everything (at least in intention). But we are not you. We are not gifted 'musicians'. We are only poor sinners, the weakest of the weak. Besides, the strongest of men remains radically unequal to what is required to be 'perfect as the Father is perfect' (Matthew 5:48). You call us to a participation in the divine nature (2 Peter 1:4), to intimate communion with the Blessed Trinity. It is a question on ontology, of being. We are not so exalted, neither is any creature, even the highest of the angels.

THE GIFT OF THE SPIRIT

But it is precisely because you know this that you have given us the extraordinary gift of your own Spirit. You have confided the work of our sanctification to the Holy Spirit because it is entirely a work of love. Who could effect this better than the One born eternally of the Love that unites you with the Father? Thus by the action of the Spirit, having become children and coheirs in the Son, we enter into the prodigal exchange of knowledge and love that operates among the Persons of the Blessed Trinity, which is intimate life with God, the ultimate reality of being. To this end, by sanctifying grace, we are raised to a level of divine being in the depths of our heart. Through the theological virtues of faith, hope and charity infused in us by our baptism, we have the power truly to know God with the knowledge he has of himself (even if obscurely in this life), and to love him truly with the love with which he loves himself. Let us try to understand that it is a question not of something ersatz or imitative, but of *divine* knowledge and love. This knowledge and this love are one and unique. In the final analysis, it is God who knows and loves himself in us; that is to say, God lives the life proper to himself in us. And yet it is we who live this life. This is God's incredible gift. But this gift is received in our human nature that is so limited and so wounded by sin (2 Corinthians 4:7). We are like children into whose hands has been put the *Summa* of St Thomas. We know only how to name the letters or, at most, to read a few words. Our effort to live our divine life, as long as it is enlightened only by the obscure light of faith (so precious, yet so obscure in its sublimity) and by reason, can only be very imperfect. And even more as our wounded nature remains, which darkens our mind and puts a thousand obstacles between our will and our acts. In the end, God alone is as exalted as God. The Holy Spirit alone can heal us and enable us to live according to the fullness of grace that we have received. But not only in heaven. Here and now. We are children of God. We want, we must live as children of God. Is not our entire life one long birthing into divine life? A new creation but one that cannot be made without our co-operation?

This, then, is the drama. On one side our fragile liberty, our chaotic spirit, deafened by the noise of senses and the world. On the other, the marvellous life that we bear in ourselves, divine, eternal life, quickened by the Holy Spirit. The Holy Spirit is not something that resides passively in us. It is Love, Life, Light, because it is God. In us it is the principle of love and light. Not only is it given us to participate in the divine nature in the sense of a wondrous ontological enrichment, but it also works constantly in us through impulses in the will and through illumination in the intellect, helping us to live according to who we really are. 'For all who are led by the Spirit of God are children of God' (Romans 8:14).

DOCILITY TO THE SPIRIT

Here is the answer: to allow ourselves to be led by the Spirit (Galatians 5:16), to allow ourselves to be transfigured by the

Spirit into the image of Christ (2 Corinthians 3:18), to live according to the Spirit (Galatians 5:25), freely. We are able to block the Spirit's activity, to grieve the Holy Spirit (Ephesians 4:30). The Spirit does not act like a tyrant. And he does not treat us like automata. His activity is profound but discreet. He invites, he does not impose. He does not take away our freedom, he makes us free.

Here we see the importance of docility to the Holy Spirit and also its difficulty. Docility enables us to enter a new level of reality. It is not to be taken for granted. It is to be learned slowly in a continual deepening of our listening, our receptivity and responsiveness. With the gift of sanctifying grace to help us, we have received a new sensitivity as part of the necessary equipment to live our lives as children of God: a sensitivity to the activity of the Spirit. Just as a painter who has been given a special sensitivity to visual beauty is particularly receptive to this form of beauty, so the child of God has a sensitivity, a particular receptivity in regard to the movements and lights of the Holy Spirit.

There are all sorts of electrical waves that travel through the atmosphere around us. They escape our notice because we do not have an organ to detect them. We need a radio or television to catch these waves and to receive the messages they carry. In the same way, we need special equipment to perceive the movements of the Spirit, an ear especially adapted to its particular music. The Fathers speak of the sails of the little boat, the soul, that enable it to catch the breeze of the Spirit. Every image is inadequate. It must not over-materialise these realities that are so subtle and so delicate.

Human virtues are habitual dispositions that render the person docile to the voice of reason. There are habitual dispositions that render us docile to the Holy Spirit. They are there, in our soul, because they are not acquired by effort. They are given us through the Spirit, by the Spirit, when the Spirit is given to us. And so they are called the gifts of the Spirit.

They are named for the most characteristic activities of the Spirit: wisdom, understanding, counsel, strength, knowledge, godliness, fear of the Lord (Isaiah 11:2–3). By his activity, the Holy Spirit produces in us the same attributes that Jesus sketched in broad outline in the Beatitudes: poverty of spirit, hunger for justice, meekness, mercy, tears, purity of heart, peace – the face of Christ, of Love incarnate.

None of these lists is exhaustive. They only point to certain habitual characteristics of an essential element that is certainly able to manifest itself otherwise (at least in detail). Also, in certain individuals, one gift will be given at one time, at other times another. The active person will not be moved by the Spirit in the same way as the contemplative.

What is essential is that each person be docile to the particular activity that the Spirit exercises within them. The chords that resonate within them at the touch of the Spirit sound a theme that becomes part of the harmony of the melody of the Body of Christ in its totality. But the Spirit alone knows what this music is, and makes it. To be sure, we listen, and we are able to perceive its beauty to a certain degree and rejoice in its utter harmony. But the essential thing for us is to do all we can to make our note beautiful and in tune – so that we will sing our own theme and not that of someone else.

10

The Interior Master

THE SPIRITUAL LIFE

What is the spiritual life? It is not the life of a disincarnate spirit. It is the life of the Spirit of God incarnated in the life of a human person, according to all the capacity of his or her being (because 'the body [also] is for the Lord' (1 Corinthians 6:13)). We are spiritual persons, in the Christian sense of the word, in the measure that we live according to the Spirit and that the Spirit lives in us. 'Anyone who does not have the Spirit of Christ does not truly belong to him' (Romans 8:9). I will even say that we *are* according to how we live in the Holy Spirit. The Spirit enables us to live the life of God. And God is Reality: the only true reality and the whole of reality. To have a spiritual life does not restrict our field of vision to a part of reality. It enlarges it to embrace the whole of reality in all its dimensions.

More often, we are terribly myopic. We live at the most superficial level of our being. We act as if our ordinary conscious life were our only life. We reduce it even more to conscious life conceptualised by our cultural conventions, excluding everything that is not quantifiable or contained within a rationalist agenda. History, art, the wisdom of millennia of so many other civilisations, show us that there is infinitely more in the human person and in reality. To take one example,[1] not the most important, but one that is familiar today, depth psychology has shown us that we also have in us a preconscious and unconscious life, more extensive than and as powerful as conscious life. Its structure, its law and logic, are completely different from those of conscious life. Similarly there is a spiritual life in us. Not – to follow the image[2] – constituted at another level below unconscious life, but encompassing the entire being of the person, conscious and unconscious. It is more extensive than everyday human life and it opens onto the immense spaces of divine life. It too has its structures and its laws, very mysterious to us. However, the experience of spiritual people across the centuries has given birth to a certain empirical knowledge of the laws of this life. And above all, the Spirit of Christ is our guide, and gives us some light.

The spiritual life ought to be the congenital milieu of the life of the monk – of every person, for that matter, because it is none other than the milieu of faith. This life ought to give us the perspective by which we establish priorities according to the rule of eternity. These judgements ought to be made in the light of the Spirit. Its logic ought to be the logic of the Spirit, that is to say, the logic of Love that directs the saints and sometimes makes them so disconcerting for us. Too often we judge according to the criteria of the short-sighted and self-absorbed world.

THE FOLLY OF FAITH

Our eyes receive images of things reversed: the ceiling is on the bottom and the floor is on top. It is thanks to a further operation that the image is put right and that we see the ceiling up and the floor down. In the same way, faith reverses the image of reality with which reason presents us. 'It is the poor who are happy. Death is the door to life. To lose life through love is to save it.' We have to become used to making the constant readjustment. Otherwise we see the floor on top and the ceiling on the bottom. We are fooled by the collective illusion of an unbelieving, materialist world, centred on little me. 'For God's foolishness is wiser than human wisdom, and God's weakness is stronger than human strength' (1 Corinthians 1:25). 'We are fools for the sake of Christ,' says St Paul (1 Corinthians 4:10). Let us become fools with that sort of folly (1 Corinthians 3:18). All of our wisdom is based on the folly of the Cross, which turns human wisdom upside down (1 Corinthians 1 and 2). Perhaps we talk too much about the wise equilibrium of our life. We forget that humanly speaking you have to be a fool to embrace it! 'I came to bring fire to the earth' (Luke 12:49).

DRIVEN BY THE SPIRIT

Remember that the Spirit 'drove' Christ into the desert (Mark 1:12). 'And the Spirit immediately drove him out into the wilderness. He was in the wilderness forty days, tempted by Satan' (Luke 4:1–2). The Statutes tell us that it is with spiritual arms that he conquered the devil and his temptations (Statutes 0. 2. 10). It cannot be otherwise for us who must follow him. The measure of testing in solitude is a work of the Spirit. The temptations of the desert can be overcome only with the arms of the Spirit (see Ephesians 6:10–17).

Certainly natural wisdom is inadequate at the beginning of a monastic vocation – and in the middle and at the end! Only the light of the Spirit can make faith penetrating enough. Only the Spirit of Love is able to sensitise us to the attraction of God and give to our love the necessary strength and intensity effectively to prefer Christ to everything, and to follow him into the desert.

THE INTERIOR MASTER

'Living in the school of the Holy Spirit', our founding Fathers little by little discovered the form of our life. For 'school', read 'master'. We have already recalled the necessity of being led by the Spirit – God alone knows where he will lead us to live and to 'savour the things of the Spirit' (Statutes 4. 33. 2).

The text of St Paul to which this phrase refers is in Romans 8:5: 'Those who live according to the Spirit set their minds on the things of the Spirit.' But it is the Vulgate that probably inspired the redactors of the Statutes: *spiritualia sapiunt*. They taste what is spiritual. It is the expression of a certain connaturality, an instinct born of a certain community of being, a certain being at home with the things of the Spirit that characterises the 'spiritual' person, led, taught by the Spirit. Taste implies direct experience, a certain fruition of that which is spiritual, of that which comes from God through the Spirit. This teacher does not teach through exterior words. He lives in us (2 Timothy 1:14), in the temple of our body (1 Corinthians 6:19), in our inmost heart (Galatians 4:6). From there he leads us into the fullness of truth (John 16:13), he guides us, consoles us, illumines us, sets us aflame with his love (Romans 5:5). 'But you have been anointed by the Holy One, and all of you have knowledge' (1 John 2:20).

We have come to the Charterhouse to seek God. But only the Spirit can search 'the depths of God' (1 Corinthians 2:10). It is the Spirit who reveals the hidden and mysterious wisdom of God that St Paul promises to Christian adults, wisdom completely different from that of the world.

> Now we have received not the spirit of the world, but the Spirit that is from God, so that we may understand the gifts bestowed on us by God. And we speak of these

things in words not taught by human wisdom but taught by the Spirit, interpreting spiritual things to those who are spiritual. Those who are unspiritual do not receive the gifts of God's Spirit, for they are foolishness to them, and they are unable to understand them because they are spiritually discerned. Those who are spiritual discern all things, and they are themselves subject to no one else's scrutiny. 'For who has known the mind of the Lord so as to instruct him?' But we have the mind of Christ. (1 Corinthians 2:12–16)

The wisdom of God, the mind of Christ – it is the Spirit who is their source. Let us look honestly at ourselves: by what spirit do we habitually allow ourselves to be guided in our actions, our choices, our judgements, our desires? By the Spirit of Christ? Or by our vanity, our egotism, our pride, our touchiness, our childishness; in the terminology of St Paul, by the flesh?

SILENCE

In the Statutes we find wise and practical teaching to help us towards a life governed by the Holy Spirit. They emphasise the importance of silence.

Exterior silence first. We must protect it for the sake of 'devotion to the Holy Spirit dwelling within' us – in ourselves and in others. 'Long and uselessly protracted conversation is thought to grieve the Holy Spirit more' (Statutes 2. 14. 4).

But even more important is *interior silence*. The criterion for judging whether to admit secular information is listening to the Spirit. 'Let each one, therefore, listen to the Spirit within him, and determine what he can admit into his mind without harm to interior converse with God' (Statutes 1. 6. 6). This is but one example of the attitude of attentive listening, an attitude of interior receptivity, of pliancy and flexibility under the activity of the interior Master, who would set everything aside that might suppress his voice.

> The longer he lives in cell, the more gladly he will do so, as long as he occupies himself in it usefully and in an orderly manner, reading, writing, reciting psalms, praying, meditating, contemplating and working. Let him make a practice of resorting, from time to time, to a tranquil listening of the heart, that allows God to enter through all its doors and passages. (Statutes 1. 4. 2)

The entire doctrine of guarding the heart is implied here. It is very important and can go a long way. Our silence is not something negative, but a form of attentiveness, a positive receptivity. It is rightly compared to the figure of Mary of Bethany seated at the feet of Jesus, giving all her attention to his word. In his silence, the monk opens himself to the Word in *lectio divina*, in prayer, in the simple gaze of faith that receives God in all his creatures.

A life of prayer without interior silence is an impossibility.[3] This silence enables us completely to forget our interior conversation, our ideas and our selves, to enter into the silence of God who is fullness of life, of light and love, and where a single Word is spoken in Love, the Word who conducts us into the inaccessible light of the Father.

WHERE DOES THE SPIRIT LEAD US?

> Who continues faithfully in his cell and lets himself be moulded by it, will gradually find that his whole life tends to become one continual prayer . . . Cleansed in the night of patience and having been consoled and sustained by assiduous meditation of the Scriptures, and having been

led by the Holy Spirit into the depths of his own soul,
he is now ready, not only to serve God, but even to cleave
to him in love. (1. 3. 2)

It is not the material cell itself that teaches us, but rather
it frames a space of solitude and silence that allows us to
listen and to be taught by the Spirit. The result of this
teaching is first of all the continual prayer that the Desert
Fathers so prized: a constant attentiveness to God and a
constant movement of the heart towards him.

We know that prayer is beyond us. In its deepest reality it
is a groaning of the Spirit in us that God alone truly understands (Romans 8:26). Let us be certain that prayer is a gift
of the Spirit. No one can say that Jesus is Lord except
through the Spirit. This is true at the highest level of pure
prayer of which the Statutes speak. 'Let our heart then be a
living altar from which there constantly ascends before God
pure prayer, with which all our acts should be imbued'
(Statutes 1. 4. 11). This prayer is the most perfect fruit of
faith and love, and leads to the most intimate union with
God possible on this earth.

The last phrase in our text refers to this mystical reality
when it describes the purpose of the Spirit's activity as the
ability 'not only to serve God but even to cleave to him'. In
the thought of William of St Thierry[4] in which we find this
citation, it is a question of contemplative repose *par excellence*
of the person who is becoming a single spirit with the Lord (1
Corinthians 6:17). It also tells us something of the spiritual
journey: through the grace of the Holy Spirit the monk is
introduced into the depths of his heart and it is in this way
that he is one with God; and it is there that he meets him.
The way to God passes through a profound experience and
a transfiguration of self. We know that the heart here signifies
the centre of personal integration of human faculties
(intellectual, emotional and even physical), the source of all

human and spiritual vitality. It is the place of spiritual combat. To enter into the depths of the heart signifies the way through which consciousness is freed from its idols, stripped of its layers of the dead skin of egotism, pride and illusion, and descends to the centre of its being in humility, truth and, finally, love, to find the place of God; the place where springs the pure water of the creative Love of God. 'Here in [solitude and silence] is acquired that eye, by whose serene gaze the Spouse is wounded with love; that eye, pure and clean, by which God is seen . . . Here God rewards his athletes with the longed-for prize: peace that the world does not know, and joy in the Holy Spirit' (Statutes 1. 6. 16). This joy of love 'has been poured into our hearts through the Holy Spirit that has been given to us' (Romans 5:5).

'Thus, with the Lord's help, we may be enabled to attain to the perfection of love – which is the aim of our Profession and of the whole of monastic life – and through it, to obtain beatitude eternal' (Statutes 0. 1. 4).

APPENDIX: FROM *THE GOLDEN EPISTLE* OF WILLIAM OF ST THIERRY[5]

As to the basic desire, first of all the object of desire should be considered, then the extent to which it is desired and the way in which it is desired. If a man's basic desire is for God he should examine how much and in what way he desires God, whether to the point of despising self and everything which either exists or can exist and this not only in accordance with the reason's judgement but a loving desire of the soul, so that the will is now something more than will: love, dilection, charity and unity of spirit.

For these are the degrees of the love of God. 'Love' is a strong inclination of the will toward God. 'Dilection' is a clinging to him or a union with him; 'charity' is the enjoyment of him. As for 'unity of spirit' with God, for the man who has his heart raised on high, the perfection of the will lies in its ascent towards God: not only does the soul want what God wants, but such is his loving desire, can I say, the perfection of his desire, that it cannot want anything but what God wills.

Resemblance to God is the whole of the saints' perfection. To refuse to be perfect is to be at fault. Therefore the will must always be fostered with this perfection in view and love developed. The will must be prevented from dissipating itself here and there on foreign objects, love preserved from fading away. For to this end alone were we created and do we live, to be like God; for we were created in his image.

There is however a likeness to God which is lost only with life itself, a likeness inasmuch as one is a living being ... But there is another likeness, one closer to God, inasmuch as it is freely willed and it consists in virtue. It occurs when the *rational soul* burns to imitate the Supreme Good by the greatness of its virtue, and the unchangeableness of the divine eternity by its constant perseverance in good.

In addition to this there is yet another likeness to God. It is so close in its resemblance that it is styled not merely a likeness but unity of spirit. It makes man one with God, one spirit, not only with the unity which comes of willing the same thing but again, because I do not know a truer expression, of a virtue which is incapable, as has already been said, of willing anything else.

It is called unity of spirit not only because the Holy Spirit brings it about or inclines a man's spirit to it, but because it is effectively the Holy Spirit himself, the God who is Charity. It comes about when he who is the Love of Father and Son, their Unity, Sweetness, Good, Kiss,

Embrace and whatever else they can have in common in that supreme unity of truth and truth of unity, becomes for man in regard to God in the manner appropriate to him what he is for the Son in regard to the Father or for the Father in regard to the Son through unity of substance. The soul in its happiness finds itself standing midway in the Embrace and the Kiss of Father and Son. In a manner which exceeds description and thought, the man of God is found worthy to become certainly not God but *what* God is, that is to say man becomes through grace what God is by nature.

11

The Discernment of Spirits

The spiritual art consists entirely in allowing ourselves to be led by the Spirit. This assumes that we are capable of recognising the movements of the Spirit. Not every spirit comes from God. Discernment is imperative (1 John 4:1). The formation of a solitary monk requires a progressive initiation in discernment. This is done in the first place through the help that the young monk receives from his spiritual father in the discernment of his own spirits, which takes places regularly. But a broader consideration can help form our judgement.

DISCERNMENT OF SPIRITS IN THE BIBLE

In reality, people are subject to a number of influences. It is part of our nature to be exposed to them – biological, physiological, psychological, spiritual. The social and familial milieu in which we are immersed has a profound effect on us, and, even though we react, we invariably retain that 'something' made up of family traits and racial characteristics. At each moment of our lives are attracted, prompted, restrained, impelled by multiple impressions coming from inside and outside, just as the waves of the sea toss a boat. Our freedom responds, but our decisions are always marked by all of these influences.

THROUGH THE OLD TESTAMENT

These influences are not entirely neutral. The first pages of the Book of Genesis reveal the existence of the personal power of evil, Satan, who incites human beings into disobeying the commandments of God (Genesis 3). Adam is fallen. Human harmony is broken. Lust is let loose, the flesh is at war with the spirit. Social and political life, the exterior projection of the struggles of light with darkness, divide the human heart.

But God does not leave the field free for the Adversary. The Spirit of God also influences us, directly or indirectly. Throughout the Old Testament, this activity changes from a more or less external influence (for example, in the judges, warriors, etc.) to a more and more interior one. The ultimate hope is that the Spirit will write the law of God in the depths of the human heart so that it will be accomplished freely and fully (Jeremiah 31:33).

THE SYNOPTICS

Christ, born of the Virgin Mary through the overshadowing of the Spirit, is a sign of contradiction that reveals the secret of hearts. His mere presence forces a discernment, it requires a choice.

The first movement of the Spirit who descends on Jesus at his baptism is to lead – in Luke's account, or 'drive' in Mark's – him into the desert to be tempted by Satan. On the threshold of his public mission, Jesus is confronted with the person of the Adversary beneath the temptations to greed, to celebrity, to power, to tempt God. At the same time, it is made clear that the ways of the Spirit, those that undergird life in the Son of God, are contingent on the Father's initiative, nourished by this absolute dependence, completely welcoming his hidden role, poor, but bearing salvation for all, the role of the Servant of the Lord. All his work will be to lead people to recognise these ways of the Spirit (see the Sermon on the Mount, Matthew 5) and to exercise this choice.

The 'Jews', for the most part, do not know how to discern the activity of the Spirit in the words and miracles of Jesus. They see the activity of Satan (Matthew 12:24). It is the sin against the Holy Spirit, against the light itself (Matthew 12:31–3).

In effect, the signs Jesus does are something mysterious and hidden. They are not clearly seen except by the poor and simple. They offend the proud and worldly and provoke their rejection. These signs do not transform the world and they do not obtain paradise here and now.

In Peter's confession at Caesarea that Jesus is the Christ, the Son of God, the forces of opposition are very much in evidence. It is the Father who reveals the identity of his Son to Peter. But when Jesus speaks of the suffering and death that await him at Jerusalem, Peter cannot accept this idea and begins to rebuke him. At which Christ unmasks the presence of the Adversary behind Peter's words. ' "Get behind me, Satan! You are a stumbling block to me; for you are setting your mind not on divine things but on human things" ' (Matthew 16:21–3). Divine light and Satanic confusion follow each other closely and contend for Peter's mind, precisely in regard to what is paradoxical and repulsive for people in the work of Christ: the Cross. Here is a criterion that will always remain invaluable for discerning the disciple of the Lord (Matthew 16:24).

The thoughts of God are not our thoughts (Isaiah 55:8–9). The disciples' temptation is to want success at a merely human level, precise dates and obvious signs (Mark 13:4). But the Kingdom of God is the fruit of sacrifice. It is not obvious to the eye (Luke 17:20). It is among us (17:21) and grows slowly and secretly like a seed planted in the earth (Mark 4:26–9).

Jesus gives a simple rule for discerning between false prophets and those sent by God: ' "You will know them by their fruits . . . every good tree bears good fruit, but the bad tree bears bad fruit" ' (Matthew 7:16–17).

The parable of the sower (Matthew 13:3–23) shows us the characteristic of the person who receives the Word of God and bears fruit, in contrast to those who bear no fruit: the latter do not understand the Word or persevere at the moment of testing, or the Word of God is choked by the cares of the world and the lure of wealth.

Sometimes discernment is very difficult; the good and the bad are inextricably mixed. We must leave the darnel among the wheat until harvest (Matthew 13:24–30).

Christ puts us on guard against the spirits who return to a house that is ' "empty, swept and put in order . . . and the last state of that person is worse than the first" ' (Matthew 12:43–5). This is a reality of the spiritual life, above all of the solitary. A false peace in the absence of occasions of sin and maintained by a tactical retreat by the Adversary, rather than by positive virtue, is followed by a violent return of hurtful passions. The house cannot stand against the storm unless it is built on the rock of Christ, on the Word of God and inhabited by his Spirit, that is to say, his Love. There is a danger, above all for the beginner, of an 'emptiness' that is only an emptiness and not an expression of personal love for the Lord and our neighbour, based on an ascetic, moral, tested and prudent life.

One day, Jesus' disciples were unable to heal a person tormented by an evil spirit. Jesus cast out the demon. The disciples wanted to know why they could not cast it out. Jesus said to them, ' "Because of your little faith. For truly I tell you, if you have faith the size of a mustard seed, you will say to this mountain, 'Move from here to there', and it will move; and nothing will be impossible for you. But this kind does not come out except by prayer and fasting" ' (Matthew 17:20–21). Faith, prayer, fasting.

Jesus heals the sick and casts out demons. Behind the demons stands the person of Satan, the Prince of this world, which is in bondage to him. Christ comes into the world not only to exercise mercy, but also to do battle with evil. Mark describes the exorcisms in the language of combat (Mark 1:23–7; 3:27). The healings and exorcisms are manifestations of the time of salvation and of the destruction of Satan's kingdom (Luke 11:20). It is in faith in this power that Anthony and the first monks deliberately sought combat with the Adversary in the desert.

ACTS

We can see the activity of the Spirit in the apostolic Church. The Spirit asserts itself in an obvious way through its initiative, strength and miraculous signs. The discernment is relatively easy.

ST PAUL

The picture painted by St Paul is more nuanced. Christian life is a perpetual discernment, an always watchful attentiveness, with the dual concern of guarding against sin and continually searching for the best. To discern the Spirit is to discern the will of God for a person in the real world so that all of life is adoration (Romans 1:28; 2:18). This requires a transfiguration of our being. We thus see according to what is. 'I appeal to you therefore, brothers and sisters, by the mercies of God, to present your bodies as a living sacrifice, holy and acceptable to God, which is your spiritual worship. Do not be conformed to this world, but be transformed by the renewing of your minds, so that you may discern what is the will of God – what is good and acceptable and perfect' (Romans 12:1–2).

The capacity for discernment grows as love grows. It is the 'tact' of love, not the 'cold' judgement of reason. 'That your love may overflow more and more with knowledge and full insight to help you determine what is best' (Philippians 1:9–10). There is a clarity and maturity in Christ (Ephesians 4:13) that comes with the practice of love in the Church. 'We must no longer be children, tossed to and fro and blown about by every wind of doctrine, by people's trickery, by their craftiness in deceitful scheming. But speaking the truth in love, we must grow up in every way into him who is the head, into Christ' (Ephesians 4:14–15). The author of the Letter to the Hebrews expresses the same idea. 'Solid food is for the mature, for those whose faculties have been trained by practice to distinguish good from evil' (Hebrews 5:14).

This perfection of Christian maturity, if it presupposes a marshalling and continual exercise of all of our personal resources, is not the resourcefulness of this world but of the Spirit, because it consists in penetrating the depths of the divine. 'No one comprehends what is truly God's except the Spirit of God. Now we have received not the spirit of the world, but the Spirit that is from God, so that we may understand the gifts bestowed on us by God' (1 Corinthians 2:11–12).

This discernment of spirits is not made by all Christians but by those whom Paul calls 'perfect' or 'spiritual'; not that they constitute a privileged class that has found and achieved 'perfection', but, on the contrary because, having had a genuine spiritual experience, they know how to discern an invitation to perfection within the concrete circumstances of existence. In addition, their sensibility is not simply an ordinary grace, it is the fruit of a charism.

This charism is not necessarily spectacular. It can be

discreet but effective through its incisiveness, certainty and clarity, without being in the least extraordinary. The importance of the charism is not that it is unusual but, rather, is in its fruitful and constructive character. In St Paul, discernment is associated with the charism of prophecy[1] and seems with it to constitute a distinct group like the gift of tongues and their interpretation. Prophecy and discernment reveal the secrets of hearts, and it is here, for Paul, that their value lies. Reacting to the Corinthians' mania for the gift of tongues, he opposes to the small profit that the community draws from this incommunicable gift, the fruitfulness of prophecy and discernment: 'But if all prophesy, an unbeliever or outsider who enters is reproved by all and called to account by all. After the secrets of the unbeliever's heart are disclosed, that person will bow down before God and worship him, declaring, "God is really among you" ' (1 Corinthians 14:24–5).

THE CRITERIA OF DISCERNMENT:
ST PAUL

According to St Paul, the discernment of spirits is based on the gospel precept: the tree is judged by its fruits. He gives many examples of these fruits. As he is dealing with real life, we must not expect a neatly ordered account. The activity of the Spirit is perceived at work with all the complexity of life. However, it seems to me that we can distinguish (a little artificially) among three fundamental principles of discernment: truth, power, love.

1. TRUTH

Confessing Christ
The principal truth is the identity of Christ. All of Paul's

faith and mission are founded on the manifestation to him on the road to Damascus of the Lord in his glory and his identification with the Church (Galatians 1:15–19; 1 Corinthians 15:3–8). Also for him, the supreme criterion for the activity of the Spirit is the attitude towards Christ. 'No one speaking by the Spirit of God ever says "Let Jesus be cursed!" and no one can say "Jesus is Lord" except by the Holy Spirit' (1 Corinthians 12:3).

Light and Peace
Born of truth, the works of the Spirit bear the mark of light and peace.

> For once you were darkness, but now in the Lord you are light. Live as children of light – for the fruit of the light is found in all that is good and right and true. Try to find out what is pleasing to the Lord. Take no part in the unfruitful works of darkness. (Ephesians 5:8–11)

> And the spirits of prophets are subject to the prophets, for God is a God not of disorder but of peace. (1 Corinthians 13:32–3)

> To set the mind on the flesh is death, but to set the mind on the Spirit is life and peace. (Romans 8:6)

> For the kingdom of God is not food and drink but righteousness and peace and joy in the Holy Spirit. (Romans 14:17–18)

2. POWER

The Holy Spirit manifests itself through signs of power:[2] miracles, unusual charisms, confidence in bearing the Word of God, courage under persecution (1 Thessalonians 1:4–5;

Romans 15:18–19). The Gospel is founded not on human wisdom but on the power of the Spirit (1 Corinthians 2:4–5).

3. LOVE

Now the works of the flesh are obvious: fornication, impurity, licentiousness, idolatry, sorcery, enmities, strife, jealousy, anger, quarrels, dissensions, factions, envy, drunkenness, carousing, and things like these. I am warning you, as I warned you before: those who do such things will not inherit the kingdom of God.

By contrast, the fruit of the Spirit is love, joy, peace, patience, kindness, generosity, faithfulness, gentleness, and self-control. There is no law against such things. And those who belong to Christ Jesus have crucified the flesh with its passions and desires. If we live by the Spirit, let us also be guided by the Spirit. (Galatians 5:19–25)

For as long as there is jealousy and quarrelling among you, are you not of the flesh, and behaving according to human inclination? (1 Corinthians 3:3)

The Spirit is the gift of God's love (Romans 5:5). It engenders love alone: if love is absent, the greatest works are worthless.

If I speak in the tongues of mortals and of angels, but do not have love, I am a noisy gong or a clanging cymbal. And if I have prophetic powers, and understand all mysteries and all knowledge, and if I have all faith, so as to remove mountains, but do not have love, I am nothing. If I give away all my possessions, and if I hand over my body to be burned, but do not have love, I gain nothing. (1 Corinthians 13:1–3)

Love spontaneously adopts an authentic spiritual stance.

Love is patient; love is kind; love is not envious or boastful
or arrogant or rude. It does not insist on its own way; it
is not irritable or resentful; it does not rejoice in wrongdo-
ing, but rejoices in the truth. It bears all things, believes
all things, hopes all things, endures all things. (1 Corinthians 13:4–7)

The criteria of love are the criteria of the Spirit. It is the
same Spirit of love who inspires individuals and who is
the soul of the Body of Christ. Consequently, authentic
graces are those which 'edify' the Church (in the etymologi-
cal sense of 'build up') and contribute to its peace and unity
towards the complete fullness of Christ (1 Corinthians 14:4,
12, 26: see the whole chapter). Even though he knows his
vision was overwhelming for him, Paul realises that it fits
into a tradition which is authoritative (1 Corinthians 15:3–8).
Charity is ecclesial.

THE CRITERIA OF DISCERNMENT:
ST JOHN

John the contemplative presents us with a vision that is at
once more unified and more stark. He sees the drama of
salvation as a struggle between light and darkness. The decisive choice for each person is to accept or refuse the light in
the person of Jesus Christ, the Word of God who has come
in the flesh. In the Gospel, the presence of Jesus itself creates
the division. In the Letter of John, the Church uses this
criterion to discern those who are of Christ.

1. THE GOSPEL

Face to face with Jesus, discernment is radical and almost
immediate; the principle which moves hearts is revealed in

the full light of day. 'Whoever is from God hears the words of God. The reason you do not hear them is that you are not from God' (John 8:47). Through a mysterious connaturality, the 'children of light' (12:36) hear the voice of Christ and recognise it (10:27; 18:37). Those who do evil, who are afraid of the light (3:20), are incapable of hearing his voice (8:43). They do the works of their father, the devil (8:41 and 44).

The discourse after the Last Supper, so full of the promise of the Spirit, gives us the characteristics that enable us to discern his activity:

– The Spirit is not a property of the ego but a principle of testimony, of courage and combat (15:27; 16:8).

– The Spirit brings neither a new doctrine nor a new gospel, but reveals the riches of the word and person of the historic Christ.

> When the Spirit of truth comes, he will guide you into all the truth; for he will not speak on his own, but will speak whatever he hears, and he will declare to you the things that are to come. He will glorify me, because he will take what is mine and declare it to you. All that the Father has is mine. (16:13–14)

– The sign by which we all recognise disciples of Jesus is the love that we have for one another (13:35).

The Passion reveals in public the methods and malice of Satan and his servants. It also reveals the triumph of love on the Cross and the ways of the Spirit who guided Jesus. John, contemplating the pierced Christ delivering his Spirit to the Church (19:30) becomes aware that at this hour the Church being born receives from the Spirit the secret of discernment which Jesus possessed.

2. THE FIRST LETTER OF ST JOHN

This letter is a veritable treatise on discernment. It was written to give discernment between the true faith and heretical, 'gnostic', doctrines. It interests us particularly because it bears on the core of Christian experience, the one we try to live above all: communion with God and with our brothers and sisters, in Jesus. Communion, abiding, possession: all of these terms gesture towards the same mystery, the mystery of eternal life, which is God himself, which God communicates and which we live in the deepest and most mysterious place in our being.

John the contemplative is a great realist. To the reality of the Incarnation of the Word of God enfleshed, there must be the response of the incarnation of faith in the life of the believer. Faith is not confined to an intellectual adherence to its truths. It is a matter of 'doing what is true' (1:6), that is to say, 'to love in the light of truth',[3] and that by virtue of a principle of light and love: the Holy Spirit who is in us and who communicates the divine life.

For John, the criterion is simple. If we are the children of God we are and we act like him. Now God is justice, God is light, God is love. This love, this justice, this light are manifested in Christ. Those who are born of God walk in love, in justice, in light, in the same way Christ has walked. Those who walk in the darkness of error and untruth, in sin and hate, show that they are not born of God but of the Devil.

God	Signs of the Child of God	The Mark of the Devil
1) is *light* (1:5); in the incarnate Word eternal life is revealed to us (1:2).	– faith: belief in Christ (5:1) and confessing him (2:23) – sincerity, to recognise ourselves as sinners (1:9) – to do the truth (1:6) in love (1:7).	– unbelief (2:22) – anti-Christ – untruth – error.
2) is *just* (1:9) his justice (in the biblical sense) is revealed in Christ's work of salvation (2:1–2).	– to practise justice (2:21) – to observe the commandments (2:3–5) – to be pure as Christ is pure (3:3) – not to sin (3:9).	– sin (3:9) – the lust of the flesh, of the eyes, of the world (2:15–17).
3) is *love* (4:8, 16) gift of self and communion. The love of the Father is revealed to us in the sacrifice of Christ (4:9–10) and is communicated to us by the Spirit.	– to love God – to keep his commandment to love our brothers and sisters (4:12–17) as a child of God (5:2) as Christ has loved (2:6; 4:17) – to have complete confidence before God in prayer (3:21–22) and thus of his judgement (2:28; 3:21).	– hate – murder – fear

Instead of talking about discernment, today we are going to experience it. We will read the letter of St John and we will allow the Word of God to judge us. Is there perfect correspondence, which is our deepest truth, between what we believe and our way of being and doing? Each of us, in his secret heart, must now answer this question.

The letter comprises three parallel descriptions. In the first (1:5—2:28), it is above all communion with God who is light. In the second (2:29—4:6), with God who is justice. In the third (4:7—5:12), with God who is love. Each description recapitulates the themes of justice (or purity), love and faith, in this order, and each time at a deeper level, to the point that in the third everything has its source in Love alone.

Let us have a time of silence between the reading of each description. Let us allow the Word of God to conceive us through love (3:9).[4]

> Beloved, let us love one another, because love is from God; everyone who loves is born of God and knows God. Whoever does not love does not know God, for God is love . . . In this is love, not that we loved God but that he loved us and sent his Son to be the atoning sacrifice for our sins. Beloved, since God loved us so much, we also ought to love one another. No one has ever seen God; if we love one another, God lives in us, and his love is perfected in us. By this we know that we abide in him and he in us, because he has given us of his Spirit. (1 John 4:7, 8, 10–13)

The Anointing of the Spirit
In John, the gift of the Spirit is not, properly speaking, a criterion of discernment. It is a source of faith and love. But John even more than Paul insists on the interior character of the Spirit's activity. In the final analysis, truth does not come from any human source. The person who believes is 'taught by God' (John 6:45), is introduced into truth by the pen-

etrating action of the Spirit, which John compares to an
anointing with oil, with all that this implies of suppleness,
power, gentleness and intimate penetration. 'But you have
been anointed by the Holy One, and all of you have knowledge (2:20) . . . The anointing that you received from him
abides in you, and so you do not need anyone to teach you'
(2:27).

However, the interior light never contradicts the exterior
revelation of the Church. The source is one. 'Whoever knows
God listens to us [the Church], and whoever is not from God
does not listen to us. From this we know the spirit of truth
and the spirit of error' (4:6 – see also 5:6–9).

A Global Perspective

Notice that for John the discernment of spirits has a global
and synthetic character. It is an overall perspective in which
everything is embraced and each element is ordered according to its true value. Confessing the incarnate Word in communion with the Church, faith is also an interior experience
in the Spirit: a communion in love and intimate presence
with the divine persons, pouring forth love of neighbour in
deed and in truth. All of these gifts are given together: where
one of them is lacking, we can assume the others are too.

Contemplatives, people of prayer, are united with the inner
source of love and truth; the monk gives concrete expression
to this love for his neighbour and the world.

12

Discernment of Spirits in Monastic Tradition

It is not possible here to gather all the riches contained in the Desert Fathers. The discernment of spirits forms part of the life of every Christian and is exercised in the historical context of each age.

THE DESERT FATHERS

We will limit ourselves to the writings that relate the experiences of the first monks. The Desert Fathers were very preoccupied with the discernment of spirits.[1] By his way of life, the monk is separated from many exterior occasions of sin. Thus the struggle becomes more interior and takes place at the level of 'thoughts'; that is to say, suggestions, voluntary impulses and ideas that present themselves to the mind and solicit its free consent. The origin of these thoughts can be God (or an angel), our nature, or the Devil. Citing St Paul's text, the elders willingly recognised the activity of the demons behind temptation. 'For our struggle is not against enemies of blood and flesh, but against the rulers, against the authorities, against the cosmic powers of this present darkness, against the spiritual forces of evil in the heavenly places' (Ephesians 6:12).

Anthony went into solitude to confront the Devil on his own ground, the desert. The formation of the early monks gave an important place to identifying demons, to the knowledge of their psychology, the relationships that existed among them, etc. They spoke of them in a very simple and anthropomorphic way (for them, the demons had a more or less ephemeral body). It is only with Evagrius that a more theological approach begins to be elaborated. Nonetheless, they had a real empirical knowledge of spiritual combat and left their often acute observations on the psychology of temptation in which monks of every age easily recognise themselves.

DISCRETION

At the heart of monastic tradition we find the notion expressed by the Greek word *diakrisis* that is traditionally translated into English as 'discretion'. It has two meanings: 1) discernment of spirits; prudence in the guidance of others and oneself; 2) the sense of proportion and of the appropriate balance. The texts illuminate sometimes one, sometimes the other meaning, but the two are intimately connected.

Cassian put Abba Moses' remarks on discretion in the second conference in his collection, after the one explaining the goal which the monk seeks, and before the one on spiritual combat. The reason for this is that discretion is the one absolutely essential virtue for the monk, and especially for the beginner.

Abba Moses was concerned above all with the discernment of spirits.[2] He described an assembly of elders presided over by St Anthony, who were asked what they considered to be the virtue able to give the monk protection from the snares and delusions of the Devil, and allow him to ascend directly to the summit of perfection. Each elder suggested a virtue of his choice: love of fasting and vigils, renouncing everything, the solitude and secrecy of the desert, practice of fraternal charity, etc.

Finally, Anthony spoke:

All the practices you have mentioned are useful for those who thirst for God and desire to come to him. But when it comes to awarding them the prize, the cruel experiences and countless failures of so many solitaries do not allow it. How many of them have we seen given over to the most rigorous fasts and vigils, calling forth admiration for their love of solitude, throwing themselves into such absolute denudation, that they would not have allowed themselves to hold on to provisions for even one day, even a single coin, eagerly fulfilling the obligations of hospitality. Then, suddenly, they have fallen into illusion; they have not been able to complete the work they undertook; they have exhausted the most beautiful fervour and a praiseworthy life with an abominable end.

But we will clearly be able to recognise the virtue that is most efficacious to take us to God, if we look for the exact cause of their illusion and downfall. Now, the virtues you have named were overflowing in them; it was the absence of discretion alone that made them unable to persevere until the end. In fact, we cannot see another cause of their ruin, except that they did not have the opportunity to be formed by the elders, and so they could not acquire this virtue, which equally preserves us from two contrary excesses, and teaches the monk always to walk by the royal way and permits him to stray neither to the right by way of a foolishly presumptuous virtue and exaggerated fervour that exceeds the limits of an appropriate temperance, nor to the left towards indolence and vice and, under the pretext of a strict ordering of the body, a slothful indifference of spirit.

It is discretion, which in the Gospel is spoken of as the eye and lamp of the body: 'The lamp of your body, said the Saviour, is your eye. So if your eye is healthy, your whole body will be full of light; but if your eye is unhealthy, your whole body will be full of darkness.' In fact, it discerns all of a person's thoughts and acts, sifts and sees in the light we in fact have. If this interior eye is ill; in other words, if we lack either knowledge or trustworthy judgement and we delude ourselves through error and presumption, our whole body will be full of darkness; know that in ourselves everything, intellect and activity alike will be permeated with darkness; because vice blinds us, and passion is the mother of darkness. 'If then the light in you is darkness, says the Saviour once more, how great is the darkness!' No one ought to doubt that, if we have a judgement that is false and lost in the night of ignorance, our thoughts, and our works which derive from them as their source, will be enveloped in the darkness of sin.

All of this agrees with the principle that 'discretion is the mother and moderator of all virtues'. How is it acquired?

True discretion is bestowed only as the prize for a true humility. The proof of this will be to leave to the elders' judgement all actions and even thoughts, in such a way that one doesn't trust himself in anything, properly speaking . . .

This discipline will not only teach the young monk to walk uprightly by the path of true discretion; he will also gain a real immunity in the face of all the ruses and snares of the enemy. It is impossible to fall into illusion if he does not rely on his own judgement, but rather allows the examples of the elders to rule his life; and all the skill of the enemy cannot prevail against the ignorance of one person who is otherwise incapable of hiding through false shame any of the thoughts that are born in the heart, but hands them over for the mature evaluation of the elders, so as to know if he should allow or reject them.

An evil thought once brought to light loses its venom

immediately. Even before discretion can stop it, the hideous serpent, which this confession has, so to speak, dragged from the darkness of his underground lair, to bring it to the light . . . hastens to beat a retreat; and his pernicious suggestions can only hold sway over us to the extent that they remain hidden in the depths of our hearts. May false shame never hold back the monk.

No other vice is more likely to lead a young monk so rapidly to ruin than to despise the counsels of the elders and to have confidence in his own judgement and his personal perspective. Every vocation, even the most practical, requires a master to be properly understood. Which is all the more reason that the disciple in spiritual combat should be attentive to these hidden and mysterious powers.

DISCRETION IN THE STATUTES

We have frequently praised the Carthusian rule for its wisdom and balance: Bruno and Guigo seemed to have possessed these qualities to a high degree. The Renewed Statutes follow in this tradition when they commend discretion among the indispensable virtues of our way of life. 'Among the qualities, with which the candidate for life in solitude should be particularly endowed, a sound and balanced judgement is of prime importance' (Statutes 1. 8. 2). All other defects are more or less curable, with the grace of God. The lack of judgement is not curable: without judgement there is no foundation to build on – at least, in extreme cases, when it is a question of some sort of congenital ineptitude for reasoning and judging correctly. Faithfulness to exterior observance cannot make up for it.[3]

Ordinarily, monastic tradition requires the candidate for the solitary life to undergo a long apprenticeship in the cenobium. The monk who confronts the Adversary one-to-one must be experienced. With us, things happen differently. A life of pure solitude, even in the end, is not part of our vision. From the beginning to the end, the monk has an existence composed of solitude and community life in carefully established proportion. The young monk, therefore, 'is placed in solitude from the very beginning of his new form of life and left to his own counsel' (4. 33. 2). He must be capable of discerning the impulses of the Spirit so that he can allow himself to be led by him. This presupposes 'a mature mind that is master of itself, and knows how to embrace honestly all that follows from the best part that it has chosen' (Statutes 1. 6. 5).

The young monk is treated like an adult. 'Now no longer a child, but a man, let him not be tossed to and fro and carried about with every new wind, but rather let him know how to recogise what would please God and do it of his own free will, enjoying with sober wisdom that liberty of God's children, concerning which he will have to render an account before God' (4. 33. 2). Note how the liberty of the children of God is neither anarchy nor the leisure to do what he wants; it rather consists in recognising what pleases God and doing it of his own free will. For this to be possible there must be a certain personal consistency, a capacity to evaluate the ideas and projects that present themselves to the mind as a function of firmly held principles, and, thanks to a will that is sufficiently free from constraint, to do what one ought, as one sees it, according to God's will.

The young monk 'is not a child but a man'. This phrase gestures at an ideal. Certainly there must be a certain maturity to go into cell, but more frequently this maturity is more or less deficient in young people of our day (probably of every day, to a certain degree). The world and its ideas are undergoing rapid change in great confusion, the family background is rarely ideal, pre-monastic religious formation is inadequate. Young people reach human maturity, especially affective maturity, more slowly than formerly. They often bear deep wounds and multiple blockages. A religious vocation will not change all of this with the wave of a magic wand. But the experience of God that is at the vocation's heart provides a core around which the personality may form or reform – but little by little, through a painful fidelity to the growth of the divine embryo, through failures and trials, through a continual beginning again that arises from the confidence that faith bestows. And the thing that enables the slender plant to grow towards the sun, is the warmth of the love of God that vivifies it and attracts it to him.

But divine charity needs a human face that is more within the novice's scope. This reveals the importance of the community aspect of our life. Affective maturity cannot be realised without a minimum of human contact. The quality and sincerity of relationships between novices and the spiritual father, and among the novices themselves[4] and with the community are decisive for this maturation.

But, as it is the attraction of solitude above all that leads candidates to the Charterhouse, it happens that when they enter they dream of a more absolute solitude. They bear the constraints of our community life with difficulty, not understanding how very necessary it is. Solitude is beneficial for those whose heart is clean, peaceful and pure and who have the capacity for contemplative repose. To seek to enter it without having completed this work – work that is often painfully long – is not wise. Even those who have begun well are sometimes tempted to be free of the formation process and to be independent prematurely.

This is a classic temptation of which Cassian speaks apropos of those who want 'a presumptuous and fatal liberty'.

They are not willing at any price to cut out their old bad

habits and faults. They are no longer satisfied to endure
the yoke of humility and patience. They disdain to be
ruled by elders. They look for remote cells and they wish
to live alone so that with no one to bother them they can
have the name among men of being patient, gentle or
humble. But . . . it is not enough to say that their vices
are not corrected; they get worse.[5]

The first monasteries in Egypt were born precisely from
the desire of those ardently seeking God who grouped themselves around a spiritual father to be guided by him and to
profit from the indispensable help that obedience gives
to vanquish the most tenacious enemy of all, self-judgement
and self-love.

To grow into maturity in the liberty of a child of God, the
young monk must freely place the beneficial yoke on his
shoulders. If he has so much pride or presumption that he
thinks he is mature from the beginning, he will certainly fail.

> Let no one, however, be wise in his own eyes; for it is to
> be feared that he who neglects to open his heart to an
> enlightened guide, will lose the quality of discretion and
> go less quickly than is necessary, or too fast and grow
> weary, or stop on the way and quietly fall asleep. (Statutes
> 4. 33. 2)

Discretion requires common sense and balance. But it
does not mean settling for a bourgeois mediocrity that flees
all effort and all sacrifice. The appropriate ascesis is to be
discovered in the light of faith, according to the vigour of
the Gospel and not according to the wisdom of the world
(Matthew 5:29–30). There are circumstances which require
extreme measures. And there are personal graces.

A beginner's typical mistakes are, on the one hand, the
presumption with which he throws himself into ascetic efforts
beyond his real strength. He does not understand his own

weakness. He does not know how to support the weakness of others. And so he becomes proud, impatient, judgemental of his neighbour, then, when the straw of enthusiasm is consumed, he falls into discouragement, laxity, the desire to quit the entire enterprise. Or, second, one sees others who do not risk wearing themselves out at all. On the contrary, they are only too 'reasonable' – and slothful. This too is a failure of true discretion which clearly sees the necessity of a rigorous asceticism and a positive effort to combat the passions before entering the repose of the Kingdom of God. One does not climb a mountain without exacting labour.

Therefore let us strive with all our ability to acquire, by the virtue of humility, the blessing of discretion, which will keep us from being hurt by two extremes of excess.

For there is an old saying: Excesses meet. Too much fasting and too much eating come to the same end. Keeping too long a vigil brings the same disastrous cost as the sluggishness which plunges a monk into the longest sleep. Too much self-denial brings weakness and induces the same condition as carelessness. Often I have seen men who could not be snared by gluttony fall, nevertheless, through immoderate fasting and tumble in weakness into the very urge which they had overcome. Unmeasured vigils and foolish denial of rest overcame those whom sleep could not overcome. Therefore, 'Fortified to right and to left in the armor of justice', as the apostle says (2 Corinthians 6:7), life must be lived with due measure and, with discernment for a guide, the road must be traveled between the two kinds of excess so that in the end we may not allow ourselves to be diverted from the pathway of restraint which has been laid down for us nor fall through dangerous carelessness into the urgings of gluttony and self-indulgence.[6]

13

The Purification of the Passions

Here, then, is the young monk who is trying the monastic life and becoming acquainted with the rigours of solitude. To warn him against the temptations that will test him, the Fathers made a catalogue of the principal vices. They did not have any illusions about men. They knew that human nature is wounded. The powers of evil do not hesitate to attack the weak points, and they find much complicity within. Peace of soul can be bought only at the price of a long struggle.

The Desert Fathers' perspective was essentially practical. Their understanding of the human person was born from their experience of the spiritual life. Because of this, we have much to learn from their school, even if we are not able to take on board their more or less Platonist conception of man that is implicit in it. At the practical level, it remains true that the flesh (in the biblical sense, the weight of evil in every person, body and soul) struggles against the spirit (in every person to the extent that they are open to God, Truth and Love). The unruly passions are a sickness. Fallen humanity cannot regain health and harmony of being without purification of the passions, whose energy can then be used in the service of goodness and love; or to put this another way, a person's vital energy in its true nature becomes harmoniously integrated at all levels of being, united in love and truth.

We must not confuse this point of view with that of modern psychology that sees the full flowering of the personality solely as a function of human needs and potentials. Faith is the point of departure for the Fathers, and union with God their goal. If they must judge the effects of a passion, it is the effect on prayer that they scrutinise. Following Evagrius, the way of the monk is presented as follows:

> Faith is strengthened by the fear of God, and it in turn is strengthened by continence; this is made firm by perseverance and hope, which give birth to *apatheia* (let us say peace or purity of heart) which has charity for a child; and love is the doorway to knowledge (the knowledge of the created universe), which is crowned by theology (the mystical knowledge of the blessed Trinity); which ends in beatitude.[1]

The word that is translated here by 'continence' (*enkrateia*) is a fundamental ascetic virtue of which celibacy is only one particular form; more broadly it entails steadfastness against all the impulses of the passions. This includes the idea of a constant sobriety in regard to the use of earthly goods, without craving or anxiety, strictly according to need. Anything that enters us in peace does not risk reawakening the passions through thought or memory. In this way the foundations of a lasting peace of soul are formed.

For the Fathers, the eight principal[2] vices are: greed, unchastity, avarice, anger, sadness,[3] accidie (*acedia*), vainglory and pride. But in the considerations which follow, we are going to enlarge the Fathers' perspective to include moral elements that are neutral or good (psychologically healthy or unhealthy) of the passions in question, in the light of modern psychology.

Psychology looks at human behaviour as, in each case, adaptive or maladaptive to integrating the personality and living with others. It tries to understand the origins of attitudes which frequently are affective as opposed to voluntary. They are not an expression of bad will (therefore, subjec-

tively, vices, voluntarily adopted in contradiction of moral
and spiritual demands) but the expression of psychological
immaturity, or a deep wound, old or new.

What follows does not begin to be exhaustive; we have to
limit ourselves here to the practical human considerations
with an eye to helping the young monk to understand himself, the better to have self-control and to have more compre-
hensive insight into the way he looks at other people.
Understanding the complexity and variety of causes that
can influence behaviour, the young monk will refrain from
judging others, and thus be obedient to the gospel precept
(Matthew 7:1). Christ has commanded us not to judge our
neighbours, but to love them in all sincerity. Among the
defensive mechanisms that can be awakened by such an
enquiry is one that sees everything in others (that is really
Dom X!) and not in one's self (Matthew 7:3).

A. VICES RELATED TO LUST

1. GREED OR GLUTTONY

Thoughts[4]
The gluttonous thought suggests to the monk a speedy end
to his ascesis: it shows him his poor stomach, the risk of a
long illness, the hardness of the climate, etc. It makes him
remember his brothers who have suffered the disastrous
consequences of excessive fasts, etc.

Forms
– eagerness to begin a meal before the time fixed by the
  rule.
– pleasure in gorging oneself, whatever the quality of the
  food.[5]
– search for delectable foods.

Effects
- produces sadness and aversion to monastic discipline.
- arouses sexual desire.
- avarice, lack of poverty.

Remedies
- abstinence, fasting and prayer.
- sometimes there are affective roots that need healing.

2. IMPURITY

Thoughts
- that sexual abstinence is pointless; suggestive words and images present themselves to the mind and imagination, etc.

Forms
- illicit relationships.
- masturbation.
- sins of thought and desire.

Remedies
Gluttony and impurity are 'natural' vices: many times they are aroused apart from any desire of the will, because of the impulses and restlessness of the flesh itself in its concupiscible part. They are linked: in order to cure impurity, one must cure gluttony. Both need an exterior object if they are to be completely fulfilled and only take effect by a physical act. Thus to curb these attacks, there is a double remedy: corporeal and spiritual. Corporeal: bodily mortification, vigils, fasts, work, removing natural enticements through fleeing such occasions and by solitude.[6] Spiritual: filling the mind with good thoughts through attentive meditation of holy Scripture, etc.; occupying the imagination with worthy images; having a careful vigilance that immediately

excludes images or suggestions of impurity that present themselves;[7] lively and personal love for God, our Lord and the Blessed Virgin.

There can be an affective element in these temptations that expresses a need or a frustration of love. Sometimes, too, neuro-physiological conditioning or psychological reflexes or blockages enter the picture, when a person's sexual development has been troubled. In this case, it is through the individual's human maturation and the unification of their being that the solution can be effected. This demands time, patience and humility. The goal of perfect chastity, the expression of a love that unifies the whole personality, can only be accomplished gradually and slowly.

3. AVARICE

Thoughts
Suggested a protracted old age, the illnesses that will come, the bitterness of poverty, the shame of receiving from others what one needs, etc.

Forms
- failure to strip oneself of possessions in renouncing the world.
- taking back, with even greater eagerness, what one has renounced.
- desiring or acquiring things one did not have at all, previously.
- sometimes the desire to accumulate possessions (this can also apply to intellectual possessions) is a way of trying to gratify, through displacement, the lack of a sense of personal security or the feeling that one is not loved. In this case, healing is very difficult and demanding and one must a) be completely clear about accepting a very real poverty, and b) be trusting in opening to others and to God. The

latter can only happen in the presence of love coming from another.

Remedies
- to content oneself with what is necessary for each day, excluding all superfluity; to entrust everything with confidence to God's providence.
- to renounce all possessions without reservation.
- to destroy avarice through charity.

Charity cannot coexist with riches that one passionately reserves for one's self. Let us be ready with all our heart to distribute all that we have in cell for our own use, however insignificant this might be (books, tools, etc.) among our brothers – our time, our thoughts, our gifts also – everything.

4. SADNESS

Thoughts
Memories of past joys that plunge the soul into sadness, reminding it of joys that are no longer and could never be again, because of the life that is now his.

Forms
- it follows on frustration of desire.
- a genuine loss.
- repressed anger.

Remedies
- non-attachment to the world's pleasures, freedom from earthly goods (because sadness is born from frustration of a present or anticipated gratification).
- vigilance against daydreaming; to live in the present moment, within the cell's four walls.

ANXIETY

In this latter sense, avarice and sadness are siblings, both being sickness of the lustful part of the soul. But Cassian speaks of another form of sadness 'that gives rise to anxiety and despair for which there seems no cause'. We do not have any difficulty in recognising what our age calls anxiety, which depth psychology has identified as the core of all neurosis. The tensions of modern civilisation are such that there are few people who are not affected by it to some degree (though not at the level of intensity that is neurotic). It seems to me that there is even a kind of anxiety of solitude, at least an anxiety that is peculiar to solitude, when a person is confronted with their own nothingness and their ontological solitude in a way that ruthlessly denudes them. Spiritual 'emptiness' often has an element of this, as does accidie (*acedia*).

In its psychological form,

> anxiety is a more or less permanent and serious state of psychological tension and contracted muscles (one always accompanies the other) that extends from an uneasy restlessness to an absorbing fear and then to a distress that can be suffocating and paralysing, when a person discovers or believes himself to be in a dead-end situation that threatens, for a more or less short time, his security and his life.[8]

In extreme cases,

> they can feel pushed to rebellion or to committing an irremediable act. In which case the person seems to be caught in a 'death wish', a blind and vengeful compulsion which is an act of defiance and protest in the face of destiny and the One who controls it. But in reality, this anxiety and tension also arises from the inner conflict and the life-preserving reaction of the whole being against

the threat of death by suffocation; it entails a struggle and an effort to escape suffering and destiny and can lead the one conquered to believe that he is also a conqueror.[9]

Frequently an 'objective' solution does not exist; the person must accept poverty in faith and trust in God, in an act of abandonment to the Lord, the Crucified, who alone can effect change in love. This is the anxiety of every human being, because, to some extent, everyone is subject to the limits of his or her created being.

14

The Purification of the Passions II

B. VICES RELATED TO IRASCIBILITY

5. ANGER

Thoughts
Memory of those who have aggrieved us, the wrong they have done us; resentment against them; schemes for vengeance.

Forms
- sudden boiling over of irascibility, an impulse against those who have wronged us or who appear to us to have done so.
- a fire whose flames are nurtured within; or else they slip out through words and deeds (introverted or extroverted temperament).
- lasts a long time or else rises and immediately falls back (secondary or primary temperament).
- when it continues and turns into resentment it causes physical problems, nightmares (symbolic images of vengeful acts . . . the unconscious is impregnated with anger).

Aggression
Here we can note several characteristics of aggression of which anger is but one expression. There is a necessary distinction between healthy and unhealthy aggression.

Unhealthy aggression turns on that which frustrates it in a hostile and destructive way – on others or itself (masochism). This involves hatred of its object. By contrast, healthy and desirable aggression enables a person to confront the difficulties and dangers of existence with courage or even with audacity: to undertake something, without being certain of success; to overcome the reluctance of the flesh and its context in the service of noble ideals; to persevere until the end. Without this vital impulse no one would be able to respond to a somewhat exacting vocation. The first monks understood this: 'The rational soul operates according to nature when the following conditions are realised: the concupiscible part desires virtue, the irascible part fights for it; the rational part, finally, applies itself to the contemplation of created things' (Evagrius, *Praktikos*, 86, p. 37).

If the desire to assert and realise oneself is frustrated, if the need to receive esteem and love is not satisfied, if the person is too grievously thwarted by their environment, aggression can find outlets for its hostility, or take the form of tending towards blocking, depression, paralysing discouragement, turning in on itself, or again of inhibition, ambivalence, or anxious perfectionism.

The most serious deprivation is that of maternal love from which the infant receives social and moral constraints. It is difficult to remedy later on and it is the source of many rebellious and contentious attitudes.

An exaggerated will to power that needs to impose itself on others at any price is sometimes, with celibates, an expression of sexual frustration.

Hostile aggression can manifest itself overtly in acts or words (insults, backbiting, slander), or in a hidden way, for example, through irony, very prized by the French (as distinct from more offensive sarcasm, mockery, jeering and ridicule), at least when it bears on people and not ideas – and often ascribes malevolent or vicious intentions to others.

Humour is a more subtle form of irony. When it is used benignly by people who are very much in control of themselves, it can become a delicate form of fraternal charity that does not seek to hurt the other, but rather to heal by helping the person take the hint that their behaviour or ideas are offensive to others.

There are other hidden forms of hostility even more long lasting and sustained, more precisely focused on a particular person and in consequence more malignant and hurtful to the love of our neighbour. These are jealousy, resentment and hate.

Resentment and jealousy come from a wound of frustration inflicted by someone else, that our charity is not big enough to excuse, but they do not always necessarily degenerate into hate. Hate, by contrast, is an aggressive disposition not only felt, but consented to and willed, voluntarily accepted, and in this way it may be already committing interior murder, as St John tells us (1 John 3:15).

There is also the bad zeal that is not always without a link to jealousy. A jealous person does not share anything. Where the demands of the zealous person are untimely and intolerant they provoke, in general, an effect contrary to what is envisaged, because they reveal themselves as less inspired by love than by the desire – mingled with a certain animosity – to compel the other to do their duty even if it is no longer through love. In sum, the zealous person puts justice before love.

Remedies
- gentleness, towards one's self first of all, then towards others. If one solves one's own problems in a brutal way, one risks being brutal towards others.
- compassion. Instead of being offended by someone, to try to understand them with the heart from within.
- 'not to let the sun go down on your anger' (Ephesians

4:26). To be reconciled with your brother interiorly
and exteriorly before going to sleep; otherwise there is
the risk that anger will grow during the night in the sub-
conscious. The next day prayer and peace of heart will be
attenuated and troubled.[1]

- when your brother is irritated with you, especially if you
provoked his anger, 'leave your gift at the altar and go;
first be reconciled to your brother or sister, and then come
and offer your gift' (Matthew 5:23–4). Otherwise your
prayer will be disturbed. Pray for him and love him
(Matthew 5:44). Make some gesture of kindness to him
(Romans 12:18–21). The first obligation of charity is to
heal his irritation with you.

> When under some provocation or other the irascible
> part of our soul is stirred up, it is just at that moment
> that the demons suggest to us the advantages of solitude
> to prevent us from putting an end to the cause of our
> sadness and so being freed from the disturbance. When
> it is our concupiscence that flames up it causes us to
> seek out once again the friendly company of men, calling
> us callous and uncivil in order to bring us into contact
> with the object of our desire. But give no confidence to
> such promptings; on the contrary, follow the opposite
> course.

> Take care not to allow angry thoughts to enter or to
> give yourself over to them, by fighting inwardly with the
> one who has vexed you. Nor again thoughts of forni-
> cation, by imagining the pleasure vividly. The one dark-
> ens the soul; the other invites to the burning of passion.
> Both cause your heart to be defiled and thus you cannot
> offer pure prayer to God. Becoming the prey of discour-
> agement, you are then exposed to *acedia*. (Evagrius,
> *Praktikos*, 22 and 23, p. 22)

– use aggressive energy positively in the struggle against the passions and in the combat of prayer. Do not indulge either the body or the mind.

6. *ACEDIA*

Acedia is a Greek word that is impossible to translate into English: boredom, torpor, idleness, disgust, discouragement, etc. are some of its components. It is a state of soul *sui generis* and is linked to solitude. The monk no longer sees any meaning in his way of life. It is the heaviest temptation of all. It envelops the monk's entire being and especially darkens the intellect. It is an extreme sickness of heart. Here is a classic description:

> The demon of *acedia* – also called the noonday demon – is the one that causes the most serious trouble of all. He presses his attack upon the monk about the fourth hour and besieges the soul until the eighth hour [approximately from 10 a.m. to 2 p.m. First of all he makes it seem that the sun barely moves, if at all, and that the day is fifty hours long. Then he constrains the monk to look constantly out the windows, to walk outside the cell, to gaze carefully at the sun to determine how far it stands from the ninth hour, to look now this way and now that to see if perhaps [one of the brethren appears from his cell]. Then too he instills in the heart of the monk a hatred for the place, a hatred for his very life itself, a hatred for manual labor. He leads him to reflect that charity has departed from among the brethren, that there is no one to give encouragement. Should there be someone at this period who happens to offend him in some way or other, this too the demon uses to contribute further to his hatred. This demon drives him along to desire other sites where he can more easily procure life's necessities, more

readily find work and make a real success of himself. He goes on to suggest that, after all, it is not the place that is the basis of pleasing the Lord. God is to be adored everywhere. He joins to these reflections the memory of his dear ones and of his former way of life. He depicts life stretching out for a long period of time, and brings before the mind's eye the toil of the ascetic struggle and, as the saying has it, leaves no stone unturned to induce the monk to forsake his cell and drop out of the fight. No other demon follows close upon the heels of this one (when he is defeated) but only a state of deep peace and inexpressible joy arise out of this struggle. (Evagrius, *Praktikos*, 12, pp. 18–19)

Remedies

– diagnosis: ' "If a man recognizes *accidie* [*acedia*] for what it is, he will gain peace" ' (B. Ward (trans.), *The Sayings of the Desert Fathers*, 149 (London: Mowbray, 1975), p. 158). But in fact one characteristic of *acedia* is to obscure the vision. The spiritual father or a brother may be able to bring light to the sufferer.

– tears and hope fed by the Word of God:

When we meet with the demon of *acedia* then is the time with tears to divide our soul in two. One part is to encourage; the other is to be encouraged. Thus we are to sow seeds of a firm hope in ourselves while we sing with the holy David: 'Why are you filled with sadness, my soul? Why are you distraught? Trust in God, for I shall give praise to him. He it is who saves me, the light of my eyes and my God' (Psalm 41:6). (Evagrius, *Praktikos*, 27, p. 23)[2]

– '*acedia* is checked by perseverance and tears.'
– perseverance in cell:

The time of temptation is not the time to leave one's cell, however plausible the pretexts one may find. Rather, stand there firmly and be patient. Bravely take all that the demon brings upon you, but above all face up to the demon of *acedia* who is the most grievous of all and who on this account will effect the greatest purification of soul. Indeed to flee and to shun such conflicts schools the spirit in awkwardness, cowardice and fear. (Evagrius, *Praktikos*, 28, p. 24)

– to think of the imminence of death:

Our holy and most ascetic master stated that the monk should always live as if he were to die on the morrow but at the same time that he should treat his body as if he were to live on with it for many years to come. For, he said, by the first attitude he will be able to cut off every thought that comes from *acedia* and thus become more fervent in his monastic practices, by the second device he will preserve his body in good health and maintain its continence intact. (Evagrius, *Praktikos*, 29, p. 24)

Indeed, if we, too, live as if we were to die each new day, we shall not sin . . . when we awaken each day, we should think that we shall not live till evening; and again, when about to go to sleep we should think that we shall not awaken. (St Athanasius, *Life of St Anthony*, 19, p. 36)[3]

– continue peacefully in the healthy rhythm of prayer and work that constitutes *monastic discipline*. In this trial it is of great help in keeping your balance. It must not be abandoned.

When the holy Abba Anthony lived in the desert he was beset by *accidie*, and attacked by many sinful thoughts.

He said to God, 'Lord, I want to be saved but these thoughts do not leave me alone; what shall I do in my affliction? How can I be saved?' A short while afterwards, when he got up to go out, Anthony saw a man like himself sitting at his work, getting up from his work to pray, then sitting down and plaiting a rope, then getting up again to pray. It was an angel of the Lord sent to correct and reassure him. He heard the angel saying to him, 'Do this and you will be saved.' At these words, Anthony was filled with joy and courage. He did this, and he was saved. (Ward, *Sayings*, p. 1)

After the combat comes repose, after *acedia*, *hesychia*. For the ancient monks, if anyone wanted only to believe in God, to depend on him, to count on him, to persevere in trusting him, to live quietly, alone and silent (Lamentations 3:27–8), to accept suffering with Christ, the outcome was not in doubt. In this way, they would enter his joy and his Kingdom.

'Your faith has saved you; go in peace.'

15

The Purification of the Passions III

VICES RELATED TO VAINGLORY AND PRIDE

7. VAINGLORY

The passions of vanity and pride are closely linked. They attack the soul differently from the passions already discussed, because it is after the others are dealt with that they enter the picture.

Vainglory is more superficial than pride, but it is noxious and opens the door to its senior partner, which is a sin of the spirit. There is a sort of continuity between these two passions – it is difficult to distinguish exactly between them, but this is not important.

As indicated by the word vanity, the need to show off, to have one's exterior attributes admired by other eyes frequently masks the lack of deeper qualities that are truly worthy of admiration. Vanity is a kind of bloating that hides a vacant interior and, in the vain person, exposes a need to be well thought of – at least on the exterior level – even if he himself can hardly be deceived by this.

Human vanity is fed by all that deceives. It goes with a certain ease of manner and a subtlety of mind, in which mockery mingles with disdain, that seeks to ensure its superiority through intimidation rather than through true merit.

Belief that one is somebody is very common in France.
One makes oneself out to be of singular importance,
but frequently is merely bourgeois;
a particularly French hoo-ha.
This silly vanity is peculiar to us,
the Spanish are vain, but make a different fuss.
Their pride, to me, seems therefore, in a word,
more foolish, yes, but not so patently absurd.[1]

Thoughts

> The spirit of vainglory is most subtle and it readily grows
> up in the souls of those who practice virtue. It leads them
> to desire to make their struggles known publicly, to hunt
> after the praise of men. This in turn leads to their illusory
> healing of women, or to their hearing fancied sounds as
> the cries of the demons, or imagining crowds of people
> who touch their clothes. This spirit predicts besides that
> they will attain to the priesthood. It has men knocking at
> the door, seeking audience with them. If the monk does
> not willingly yield to their request, he is bound and led
> away. When in this way he is carried aloft by vain hope,
> the demon vanishes and the monk is left to be tempted
> by the demon of pride or of sadness who brings upon
> him thoughts opposed to his hopes. It also happens at
> times that a man who a short while before was a holy
> priest, is led off bound and is handed over to the demon
> of impurity to be sifted by him. (Evagrius, *Praktikos*, 13)

Forms

- vanity about physical, visible attributes, for example, physical beauty.
- vanity about spiritual gifts.
- vainglory born of virtue – even that one has freed oneself of it.

– vanity is ubiquitous. It takes many forms, some of them very subtle (above all with monks and nuns), sometimes quite ridiculous (except in the eyes of the conceited person, who takes himself very seriously). Here are several illustrative texts. Cassian is commenting on the novices of the 'Desert Fathers'.

> Beginners and those who make only mediocre progress in virtue and knowledge don't escape vainglory. Their voice can be a pretext for puffing themselves up – their psalmody is so melodious! – or their emaciated condition, or their noble figure; or their parents' wealth, or because they have rejected military life and honours.
>
> Sometimes it even persuades them that if they had remained in the world they would easily have acquired wealth and preferment, although there was never any guarantee of this. They become inflated with a vain hope vested in ephemeral dreams, and they become conceited over things they never had as if they had renounced them. (*Institutes*, XI, 13)

And again:

> If the demon can't make him vain by elegant and correct attire, he tries to do it by suggesting he wear a habit that is dirty, unkempt, and shoddy; if he can't conquer him through vanity, he'll get him through humility; if he can't make him pompous through knowledge and eloquence, he'll bring him to grief through his silence. If a monk fasts in front of others, he's tempted to become self-satisfied; if he hides his fasting through contempt for vainglory, it turns on him anyhow. He avoids prolonging his prayers in front of the brethren in order to escape vainglory: but when he makes them in secret without anyone to see, this too becomes a weapon of vanity. (*Institutes*, XI, 4)

The Fathers rightly compared this vice to an onion: every time you peel off one layer, another appears, and when you remove the next, there's still another one. (*Institutes*, XI, 5)

— Closer to our time (the twentieth century), there is *The Little Prince* of Saint-Exupéry, who, in his interstellar voyages, observed a conceited man on the second planet he visited . . .

The second planet was inhabited by a conceited man.

'Ah! Ah! I am about to receive a visit from an admirer!' he exclaimed, from afar, when he first saw the little prince coming.

For, to conceited men, all other men are admirers.

'Good morning,' said the little prince. 'That is a hat you are wearing.'

'It is a hat for salutes,' the conceited man replied. 'It is to raise in salute when people acclaim me. Unfortunately, nobody at all ever passes this way.'

'Yes?' said the little prince, who did not understand what the conceited man was talking about.

'Clap your hands, one against the other,' the conceited man now directed him.

The little prince clapped his hands. The conceited man raised his hat in modest salute.

'This is more entertaining than the visit to the king,' the little prince said to himself. And he began again to clap his hands, one against the other. The conceited man again raised his hat in salute.

After five minutes of this exercise the little prince grew tired of the game's monotony.

'And what should one do to make the hat come down?' he asked.

But the conceited man did not hear him. Conceited people never hear anything but praise.

'Do you really admire me very much?' he demanded of the little prince.

'What does that mean – "admire"?'

'To admire means that you regard me as the handsomest, the best-dressed, the richest, and the most intelligent man on this planet.'

'But you are the only man on your planet!'

'Do me this kindness. Admire me just the same.'

'I admire you,' said the little prince, shrugging his shoulders slightly, 'but what is there in that to interest you so much?'

And the little prince went away.

'The grown-ups are certainly very odd,' he said to himself, as he continued on his journey.[2]

Remedies

– 'I have observed the demon of vainglory being chased by nearly all the other demons, and when his pursuers fell, shamelessly he drew near and unfolded a long list of his virtues' (Evagrius, *Praktikos*, 31).

– The danger is that vainglory grows with progress in virtue. It cannot be banished by ascetic effort, any more than pride can. Only the light of contemplation and a certain experience of God can free us from the things of the world and their vanity. Only the person who has a taste for God will not look for glory except in him. Moreover, the person who has the experience that Christ lives in him or her (Galatians 2:20) attributes any virtue only to Christ.

– We must never do anything so that people will see us doing it and give us their approbation. This is what the Pharisees did (Matthew 23:5; 6:1–6). Do everything for the glory and love of God alone, in his presence.[3]

– 'How can you believe when you accept glory from one

another and do not seek the glory that comes from the one who alone is God?' (John 5:44).

– For more general remedies, see those for pride.

8. PRIDE

Thoughts

The demon of pride is the cause of the most damaging fall for the soul. For it induces the monk to deny that God is his helper and to consider that he himself is the cause of virtuous actions. Further, he gets a big head in regard to the brethren, considering them stupid because they do not all have this same opinion of him.

Anger and sadness follow on the heels of this demon, and last of all there comes in its train the greatest of maladies – derangement of mind (*ekstasis!*), associated with wild ravings and hallucinations of whole multitudes of demons in the sky. (Evagrius, *Praktikos*, 14)

Forms[4]

We must distinguish between our instinctive and domineering pride and spiritual pride.

A. Domineering pride: This is a certain focusing of aggressive tendencies that does not seek to do something against someone else or their possessions, but rather to establish a superior position with regard to someone else, to impose oneself on them, by force if need be, but not necessarily through force. This will to power and domination of the other reveals the root of pride itself, whose self-concern is absolute and who considers itself superior to all. It is this ruthless human arrogance that wishes to dominate others and the world.

The will to power is based on the animal instinct of social

hierarchy that impels an individual in a group to seek alpha status by intimidating the rest. Dominance is established as much by subtle display as by direct conflict, by body language, a tone of choice that quashes response, etc.

B. *Spiritual pride*: The pride that comes into play in the struggle for dominance is different from the will to power, just as humility and modesty, which are opposite to pride, differ from submission and obedience. Pride is more of a sin of the spirit than an instinctive impulse. One can be very proud under the guise of modesty and without having the means of imposing one's will on the other – save in the imagination through compensatory delusions of grandeur. It is enough that such persons believe themselves superior to everyone. Pride is above all having an exaggerated opinion of oneself.

This is not to be confused with positive self-respect, or an appropriate emulation, both of which are desirable for the maturation of one's being. Nor with the generosity of spirit that desires to accomplish great things. Nor with a neurotic grandiosity,[5] which up to a point is excusable when it arises from a frustration of affectivity. Pride is the pretension that illicitly attributes its merits, real or not, to itself. In reality, all our gifts – the word itself says it – come from God. We are only agents, with the obligation to provide a return on the capital we have received. We are not the owners. Pride takes credit for everything, or ascribes everything to its own deserving. In extreme form, it would take the place of God. This is the Promethean revolt of modern atheism. It is expressed in the *non serviam* that refuses obedience to God.

At a secondary level, the qualities we have acquired would not be possible without the help of others, from our social and family environments which passed on to us a wealth of development and culture accumulated by previous generations. Pride is a sort of blindness that can only see what the desire of its overblown sense of grandeur dictates.

But certainly the pride most dangerous to the monk is spiritual pride that causes him to see the origin of his good acts, real or imagined, within himself. It takes him over to the ruin of his virtue and finally, say the Fathers, to madness (a poor imitation of Nietzsche comes to mind). Pride is a drastic dislocation of right thinking, a negation of the order of things. Its ultimate experience can only be madness; in reality, it rarely goes that far.

Remedies

> Remember your former life and your past sins and how, though you were subject to the passions, you have been brought into *apatheia* by the mercy of Christ. Remember too how you have separated yourself from the world which has so often and in so many matters brought you low. 'Reflect also on this (says Christ): who protects you in the desert? Who drives away the demons who gnash their teeth at you?' Such thoughts instil humility in us and close the door to the demon of pride. (Evagrius, *Praktikos*, 33)

- The antithesis of pride is humility. Humility is modest and dispels that vanity which opens the door to pride. Its self-regard is not severe and accusatory, but balanced and realistic. It has a sense of humour, that is, a sense of the true proportions of what is real. Beholding the limitless expanse of heaven and Love nailed to the Cross, it knows itself to be insignificant and far from the goal. It does not pose or wear a mask, either to itself or to others. It reveals itself and allows itself to be known as it is. It is truth.
- Because humility cannot be acquired directly by ascetic effort, it is better to focus our effort on becoming truthful and arriving at a clear-eyed knowledge of ourselves. This

truth takes hold of us when we have an existential understanding of our nothingness and our absolute dependence
in regard to God, perceived for who he is, the All, in the
light of faith and contemplation. We must live and love
from within this truth, and this becomes possible with
faith in God-Love.

– Everything is God's grace. Grace, therefore gratuitous:
purity of heart cannot be achieved by our own efforts. It
is a gift of the divine mercy (James 1:17). Of course grace
cannot work without our co-operation. Rather, it makes
our free co-operation possible, and is brought to fruition
with our effort. 'Not I, but the grace of God that is with
me' (1 Corinthians 15:10; cf. Philippians 2:13) says Paul,
who accomplished astonishing things. 'Apart from me you
can do nothing,' says Christ in the Gospel of St John (John
15:5; cf. Psalm 126:1–2; Romans 9:16).

– The promises of God are so great that our efforts appear
insignificant by comparison.

– It is not a question of disowning God's gifts, but of recognising their source and glorifying their Creator. 'What do
you have that you did not receive? And if you received it,
why do you boast as if it were not a gift?' (1 Corinthians
4:7). Humility is not an anxious disparagement (and frequently a lie), but the activity of grace, simplicity and joy.

– The good thief, the penitent David and many others are
present in Scripture to tell us of the sovereignty of grace
and mercy. I leave it to you to undertake a reading of the
Bible with this in mind.

– Real humility is not an abstract truth. It recreates the
entire being. It springs from truth (of God, of the world,
of ourselves) lived in gentleness and simplicity of heart. It
is not obtained without a complete renunciation of the
values of this world. It is submission to superiors. It is even
obedience to our brothers and sisters, and demonstrates to
them a sincere charity that never seeks to wound or even

vex. It bears every injury and difficulty with patience. It lives in the light of God and eternity. Throughout the tradition it bears fruit in love, joy and peace.[6]

- St Augustine goes so far as to say that it is useful for the proud person to fall into manifest sin from which he may extract a remedy for his pride (*City of God*, I, 14).

- Pride is the most difficult passion to uproot. But let us be confident: what is beyond our power is possible with God, putting at his service the events of our lives, for he is also the Lord of history.

> There is a humility that comes from the fear of God, and there is a humility that comes from the fervent love of God. The first form of humility leads to fear of God; the second has joy as its principle. The first leads to modesty in all things, a right ordering of the senses, and a heart contrite at all times. But the second appears intensely simple; then the heart is lifted on high and nothing can hinder it. (Isaac the Syrian, also known as Isaac of Nineveh)[7]

- Pride never wants to submit to anyone. It knows it is always better than everyone else. It never wants to do anything other than according to its own judgement. Humility submits to God; directly through the commandments, or indirectly through the persons who represent God on earth.

The exterior appearance of submission does not reach the level of the spirit where pride is rooted. Above all, when it is demanded on threat of punishment, it generates either a passive obedience undergone rather than accepted, or else revolt and rejection of all authority. Only filial obedience, clear-eyed and freely accepted within oneself, has the power to change the human heart. In addition, the more people become aware of their personality and their rights, and acquire some culture, the less they will tolerate being treated without the deference they think is due to their position or their feelings, and without being understood before an order is given to them.

– Humility is the face through which knowledge of God comes to us, imbibed through prayer and love. Knowledge of the glory of God resplendent in the face of Christ (2 Corinthians 4:6). Our humility is the face of Christ engraved in our heart by his Spirit. This is why humility cannot be known; it is, in fact, a great mystery. The only remedy for egocentric pride is the love of Christ in us. Let us behold Christ so that we may be like him, 'gentle and humble of heart'. The Fathers loved to set Christ and Satan in opposition, humility (Philippians 2:6–11, etc.)[8] against pride (Isaiah 14:13–14, etc.). As Augustine said, 'The love of God impels us to disregard ourselves' and 'love of self impels us to disregard God'.

> Jesus Christ is a God we can approach without pride, and before whom we can humble ourselves without despair. (Pascal)[9]

> To know God without knowing our own wretchedness only makes for pride. Knowing our own wretchedness without knowing God makes only for despair. Knowing Jesus Christ provides the balance, because we find there both God and our own wretchedness. (Pascal)[10]

> For humility is the raiment of the Godhead. The Word Who became man clothed Himself in it, and through the body in which it became ours. Every one who has truly been clothed with it has been made like unto Him Who came down from His own exaltedness, and hid the splendour of His majesty, and concealed his glory with humility, lest creation should be utterly consumed by the contemplation of him. (Isaac the Syrian) [11]

16

The Purification of the Passions IV

Reading, vigils and prayer – these are the things that lend stability to the wandering mind. Hunger, toil and solitude are the means of extinguishing the flames of desire. Turbid anger is calmed by the singing of Psalms, by patience and almsgiving. But all these practices are to be engaged in according to due measure and at the appropriate times. What is untimely done, or done without measure, endures but a short time. And what is short-lived is more harmful than profitable. (Evagrius, *Praktikos*, 15, p. 20)

Small showers last long, but sudden storms are short;
He tires betimes who spurs too fast betimes.
With eager feeding, food doth choke the feeder.

(Richard II)

Thus each one, having recognised his most besetting vice, should make it his main priority to combat it, and focus all his concern and attention to see where it will attack. And he should direct all his ascetic effort against it – his fasts, vigils, meditations, prayers and tears. It is impossible to triumph over a single passion unless we understand that our personal effort and toil cannot win us the victory, although the work of purification nonetheless requires unceasing vigilance day and night. In this way

we must implore God to put an end to the attacks by
this vice. (Cassian, *Conferences*, V, 14)

Having been delivered from this vice, we turn against the
next vice which, among the others, is the most hurtful and
so on.

Smother the strongest passions in order gradually to quash
the weaker ones.

However, the passions are linked together in a hierarchy.
It is an illusion to want to fight against impurity when one
has not overcome gluttony; nor against avarice, if one has
not first of all overcome the first two. It takes a global effort;
that is to say, we must not ignore any passion while concen-
trating on the strongest.

A giant tree can be killed by cutting its roots.

Thus in order to conquer sloth, first overcome sadness;
to banish sadness, drive out anger; to quench anger,
smother avarice; to root out avarice, curb impurity; to
starve impurity, eliminate gluttony.

To combat the demons effectively we must identify them
and their habitual patterns, the psychological states
linked to the activity of divers spirits: the action of a good
spirit bestows peace; a bad one leaves disturbance in its
wake. Unmasked, they lose their power over us.
(Evagrius, *Praktikos*, 43)

The passions are like dogs that are wont to spend their
time before the butchers' stalls; they run away at the
sound of a loud voice, but if they are forgotten, they
attack like fierce lions. Set every small desire at naught,
that you may not be besieged by the vehemence of its
burning. (Isaac the Syrian)[1]

Vigilance. We must guard the door of the heart, questioning each thought that presents itself.

A monk should immediately oppose a bad thought with the thought of its corresponding virtue, thus cutting off the bad thought with the help of the good one.

But if the monk has not enough virtue for this, he should oppose one bad thought with another that cannot coexist with it (for example, vainglory and impurity). Imaginative tactic: if we are tempted with impurity, to *imagine* a vainglorious thought, because 'one idea drives away another'.

Analyse and objectify: consider separately the intellect that receives the thought, the thought in itself, the sensible object that it uses for support, the passion, and look for the sin's location. The thought will melt in the fire of analysis.

Oppose physical temptation with physical means: fast, wear uncomfortable clothes, keep vigil, recite psalms.

Beware! When the demons achieve nothing in their struggles against a monk they withdraw a bit and observe to see which of the virtues he neglects in the meantime. Then all of a sudden they attack him from this point and ravage the poor fellow. (Evagrius, *Praktikos*, 44, p. 28)

Let us not be upset by that demon who snatches away the intelligence to blasphemy and to those phantasies of a prohibited sort – too sordid to so much as mention. Nor should we let him dull our sharp eagerness. Remember this, 'the Lord knows the heart', and he well knows that even when we were living in the world we did not fall into this kind of madness. The fact is that this demon entertains the hope of causing us to cease to pray so that we might not stand in the presence of the Lord our God, nor dare to raise our hands in supplication to one against whom we have had such frightful thoughts. (Evagrius, *Praktikos* 44, p. 29)

The contents of our dreams indicate where passion is strong.[2]

'Continual concentration on the thought of God uproots the passions and causes them to flee. This is the sword that gives them the deathblow' (Isaac the Syrian).[3]

To end, let us recall a precious counsel of John of the Cross. He said that we can overcome vices in a very simple way, one more fruitful and more perfect than a direct attack. The soul instantly fights and overcomes all temptations and their power by an act of love that raises the heart directly to union with God. Thus the heart is not where the enemy would want to attack and wound it; it has escaped.

17
Discernment of Spirits in Later Tradition

With the passage of time, spiritual authors and directors of souls have developed a number of rules to clarify the question of discernment. We have become increasingly aware of the difficulty of discerning the sources of our impulses with any certainty (God, the Devil, our nature). For this it would be necessary to have an exhaustive knowledge of the human psyche, and we certainly do not have that. Gradually as we have come to know more about the influence of the unconscious, greater prudence has become essential and the whole question has taken on a different aspect. In the end, what matters is not the origin of a particular 'thought' but to know whether it is good or bad, if it should be welcomed and followed or not. And the most reliable criterion is the one the Gospel gives: the fruits of the tree. If the fruit is good, so is the tree.

The object of discernment itself is specific. Everything we are commanded by the law of God and the Church, and the obligations of our state, is certainly good. Everything that goes against this is certainly bad. But there are other situations in which the will of God is not immediately evident: for example, when we are inclined to do something that is certainly good in itself, but we do not know whether through performing it we will be unable to undertake something else that is better and more necessary, or whether the first act might not involve us in others that are less good or even bad. An infinite variety of temptations appear as good. Discernment will therefore bear on 'spirits', which may be neither evidently good or bad.

There are three categories of events requiring this discernment:

1. visions, revelations, words, etc.;
2. interior inspirations that are indistinguishable from the normal flow of consciousness;
3. general states of consolation or desolation that can indicate the will of God as it applies to a particular project (see above all the *Spiritual Exercises* of St Ignatius of Loyola).

Each of these categories can trace its origins to natural or other causes. For example:

1. morbid hallucinations;
2. an impulse that suddenly appears in awareness without apparent cause (for St Ignatius, this is a sure sign of supernatural origin) can arise from the unconscious after a long period of incubation;
3. manic-depressive temperament, states alternating between the more or less depressive or euphoric.

In addition, the natural does not exclude other influences; there is no such thing as a pure state. On the one hand, the supernatural is always the fact of this particular person with this temperament and this history. On the other, it is with words of the natural world that God most frequently writes the history of divine action with the events of 'profane' history (see the 'spiritual' reading of these events by the prophets), with our personal history, our talents, our faults, even our sins.

More precisely, we can see that Satan can take over any movement, whether its origin be natural or supernatural. Equally, the activity of grace can turn an evil inspiration to our profit (for example, when we fight and overcome a temptation).

Thus there is a tangle of very complex causes, and their discernment is very delicate work. The Holy Spirit gives certain people a charism for discernment, a sort of divine instinct which intuitively perceives whether or not thoughts and attractions have a divine origin or not. The fullness of this gift presupposes exceptional holiness, profound humility and submission to the Church's magisterium. The Curé d'Ars provides a remarkable example in recent history. No matter how great this gift may be, it does not confer infallibility. It is always possible to err in using it.

This gift in its fullness is rare, just as exceptional sanctity is rare. More often, through particular interior lights, the Spirit enhances a gift of discretion acquired by study, experience and prudence in the application of the traditional rules of discernment. These rules should be applied with great prudence because there is no rule (necessarily general) that is not capable of introducing error in a particular instance.

Here is a generally accepted list of the signs of good and bad spirits:[1]

Good Spirit	Bad Spirit
For the Intellect	
1. Truth	Falsehood
2. Nothing useless	Futile, useless, vain things
3. Clarity of *understanding* (even though sometimes the *imagination* remains clouded)	Shadows or false light in the imagination
4. Intellectual docility	Obstinately held opinion
5. Discretion	Exaggeration, excess
6. Humble thoughts	Pride, vanity

For the Will

1. Interior peace	Disturbance, disquiet
2. True, *effective* humility	Pride, false humility (in words, not acts)
3. Trust in God, mistrust of self	Presumption and despair
4. A flexible will, facility in self-knowledge	Intransigence, a hard and closed heart
5. Right intention in actions	Devious intention
6. Patience in physical and spiritual pain	Impatience in trials
7. Interior mortification	Revolt of the passions
8. Simplicity, candid truthfulness	Duplicity, deception
9. Spiritual liberty	A heart in thrall to earthly things
10. Vigilance in imitating Christ	Aversion to Christ
11. Gentle charity, goodness, self-forgetfulness	False zeal, bitterness, pharisaism

Signs of a Doubtful and Suspect Spirit[2]

1. Having definitively chosen one state, to desire another
2. To be inclined towards the unusual, the singular, things that are not consonant with one's state
3. Love of the extraordinary in the exercise of virtue
4. To look, sometimes, for extreme exterior penances
5. Too much sensible consolation
6. Continual spiritual consolation and delight without interruption
7. Tears can themselves be suspect
8. Frequent revelations to people of mediocre goodness

We must emphasise that no one of these signs is an absolute criterion. They indicate a certain probability of good or evil in an act. It is their convergence that can lead to moral certitude. Therefore it is important always to apply these indicators together.

THE SYNTHETIC VIEW

A synthetic overview alleviates, to a certain extent, the weakness of the analytic approach, which is fragmenting when applied to discernment. For in the end it is always a personal act that is under consideration, and the true meaning of this act can only be grasped when seen within the context and general orientation of the person. The same act has a different value in a beginner and in someone who is already experienced in the spiritual life. The doctor makes a diagnosis depending on the state of health of the entire person. The whole gives meaning to the part.

It is important to give full weight to the existential and historical dimensions of personal action. This is true above all when it is a matter of evaluating a person or a crucial decision such as vocation. The broad outlines of a life, and above all the fundamental choice that establishes a person's orientation towards certain high values – all this is decisive, even when a person is not yet able, perhaps will never be able, to translate these values into action in his life.[3] Liberty and virtue are realised gradually. An imperfect act, but one that moves towards greater perfection, is a better sign of spiritual health than one that objectively is more perfect, but static and perhaps self-satisfied.

No single dimension of the person should be excluded: physical, psychological, spiritual. Human beings are incarnate beings. They express their spiritual choices through their own bodies: their embodied way of being and acting.

What must be looked at is the whole which is constituted through the harmonising and unifying of all the parts of a human being, the unique integration that characterises the individual. So, on the part of the observer, there is an instantaneous and global perception – often at the very first direct contact with the person – which grasps something of the unique note that characterises the individual, without its being possible to analyse or bring into consciousness all the elements of this judgement. This is why, in concrete reality, analysis is a secondary movement, which verifies what is perceived by intuition and makes possible a more explicit synthetic perspective.

18

The Discernment of Spirits II

MODERN PSYCHOLOGY

Grace builds on nature. There is continuity between the psychological development of the human person and the life of grace. There is also disjunction, because the activity of the Holy Spirit elevates and profoundly transfigures human instincts and emotions. Let us now try to arrive at a synthetic view of human reality, by using the most elementary data of natural and divine psychology. This will help us to order things better and to understand what a prodigious work of transformation should be going on in us if we are to become disciples of Christ in all truth, and monks.

THE HUMAN PERSON

Modern psychology rests on acute observation and profound analysis, which allows understanding of many aspects of individual human behaviour. However, it does not present a single image of the whole person but several, determined in part by philosophical considerations, the assumption of positions which go far beyond the accepted insights of psychology.

Our goal here is practical. Our frame of reference is our faith. We do not accept the deterministic and pessimistic view of Freudian psychoanalysis: a human being is more than a 'psyche', he or she is also a spirit, and is able to influence psychic and other conditionings by accepting them, by refusing them, or by more or less modifying them by using human freedom in the quest of spiritual values.

Nor do we accept the subjectivist and optimistic view of Rogers, Maslow and some existentialists, for whom the goal of the human person is self-realisation, the complete fulfilment of every potentiality. This closes human beings in on themselves and limits transcendence, that is to say, the ability to go beyond themselves to objective values that are above them. Like happiness, self-realisation is not in itself an end that a human being should envision as something absolute. It is rather a side effect, a sort of bonus, arising from the realisation of higher values (love of God, service of others, justice, etc.) to which the person is dedicated. To accept the model of a human being as one that is fulfilled through the gratification of all desires is to return to the idea of the 'noble savage' of the eighteenth century.

Humans are more than human. They are fulfilled by surpassing themselves. But a human is a creature marked by the disorder of sin. It requires a long and patient struggle to put some order into anarchic desires, and to create unity in the pursuit of a noble ideal perceived by the intellect. For us, this ideal is that of the Gospel perceived in the light of faith: the ideal of love and truth in Christ, hope and immortality in God.

THE VARIED LEVELS OF LIFE

In the complex but nonetheless unified reality of the human person, there are different levels of life. These levels appear successively over time. When a superior level appears, the lesser one does not vanish; it is assumed into the superior one, transformed by its contact with it, while preserving its own nature. In the same way, our passions and motivations can have their source in one or another of these levels, or in all of them at once, and can even be in contradiction among themselves. For us to understand ourselves, it is necessary to have some idea of the structure of our being.

1. THE BIOLOGICAL AND INSTINCTUAL LEVEL

Let us talk about psycho-physiology. It is a matter of the physiological states of a living organism, linked to the most fundamental psychic activity stimulated by a reaction to some felt deficiency, or as an expression of the need of the being. At this stage we can hardly speak of a personal life, although the organism constitutes an individual.

2. THE PSYCHO-SOCIAL LEVEL

This is the sphere of the empirical self that acts on the world, on things and people. The self seeks a structure by affirming itself according to its instinctual tendencies and by reacting to the stimuli of its concrete reality here and now. At this stage the universe of such a life is already very much enlarged, but the movement of the self is primarily egocentric: it refers everything to itself. The individual is self-affirming and there is a rudimentary personal life.

Typical of this stage is judgement at the sense level of objects that are presented to the self. Through an evaluative process that is direct, immediate and intuitive, the object is apprehended as desirable or not, for me, here and now, because it is a source of immediate pleasure, in so far as it may be capable of satisfying a need or realising a potential. Felt emotion automatically follows this evaluative process, either of desire: the felt tendency of attraction to an agreeable object; or of non-desire (hate, hostility, fear): a felt tendency of repulsion in regard to the disagreeable object. Emotion is a concrete impulse towards the necessary action to approach or flee an object. The repetition of an emotion and its satisfaction generates *an emotional attitude*: a habitual disposition towards the object and the action.

In animals we find a similar direct, instinctual evaluation provoked by a physiological state resulting in a stereotyped response. The first movements in human beings are also of this nature, but they are (or can be) capable of a higher response.

3. THE LEVEL OF THE SPIRITUAL LIFE

a) The Sphere of Personal Human Life

The human spirit has the power by abstraction to go farther than the knowledge of immediately perceived sense data to understand the nature of things and the general principles of the world. It can also penetrate into the spiritual world of non-material realities that are neither discrete, nor extended in space, nor situated in time. It can construct and understand a symbolic language. It can open itself to spiritual values that transcend material and temporal life. It is not determined by sensory stimuli and it can choose the values it wishes to follow. The self can transcend itself in its aspirations towards the values and ideals to which it is consecrated. This is the sphere of human liberty. It is the sphere of personal life impossible for animals.

Typical of this level of life is *reflexive intellectual judgement* whose object is the entire process (including emotion) of felt judgement, not only under the aspect of agreeable or disagreeable, but of good or bad, for me, here and now. This judgement is based not on emotions at the sense level (which can in the meantime have their part in the formulation of judgement and, above all, in its persistence) but in the reflexive convictions of the person who transcends the limits of the empirical self, affected by sensory stimuli here and now, and who is open to spiritual and eternal values. It can correct or contradict sensible judgement (all that is agreeable and not good for me).

Thus there is the possibility of interior conflict between a felt emotional tendency towards what is desirable, and a willed tendency towards that which is judged by a free act of the will as useful and good (for example, in the choice of celibacy, obedience, etc.). This rational desire can be followed by uniquely human emotions, that is to say, a voluntary, felt tendency towards that which is judged good for me, or repulsion towards that which is judged bad for me. This voluntary emotion has repercussions on emotions at the sense level that it can more or less mobilise and focus in the same direction (this does not always happen; in any case it needs time, sometimes much time, before it happens).

The practice of intellectual judgement leads to an intellectual attitude: habitual intellectual judgement. These attitudes can evoke strong emotions but they are not based on them.

b) The Sphere of Divine Life, of the Life of the Spirit of Christ
The Christian, through union with Christ in baptism and sanctifying grace, participates in the life of Christ. We receive within ourselves a new life-principle, the Holy Spirit, new faculties for knowing with God's knowledge and loving with God's love. The light of faith opens on to the mystery of the human being and God. The unfolding of this life at once assumes and surpasses natural human life; in this we see our deepest desire fulfilled although it is hidden and cannot be realised by natural powers alone.

There is both continuity and radical disjunction. In the deepest reality of the human face is traced the image of God, thanks to an increasingly profound conformity with Christ, effected interiorly by the Spirit (2 Corinthians 3:18). Up to this point the self had struggled for self-affirmation in all the riches of its personality. The Gospel demands that we lose our life to gain it, so that it may be 'no longer I but Christ

The Vari₄

Level of Life	Needs
1. Physio-psychological, biological and instinctual life	– Organic: hunger, thirst, sleep, movement, vigilance, alimentation, elimination, respiration
2. Psycho-social sphere of empirical self spilling over in an egocentric way on the world of things and people, in their presenting reality, here and now	– To develop the self in a life of relationship with the world and those around the individual – Affiliation, affection, esteem, success, self-realisation by the self for the self
3. Spiritual a) sphere of the human spirit, of the person, the self, that transcends itself and opens itself freely to immaterial and spiritual values in a more or less self-forgetful way	– To open the self to truth, beauty (transcendent), to moral good, justice and self-forgetful love – To know and to create
b) sphere of the Spirit, of the divine – christocentric, in the church, towards the Father	– To love in deed and truth – To open to the life of Christ in us in the life of the Spirit – Communion, prayer, adoration

f our Life

Aggressive Impulses	Libidinal-Affective Impulses
– Defend self against all threats – Attacks for purpose of self-satisfaction	– Seeks every sensory satisfaction without distinction of subject and object as source of satisfaction
– Affirmation of self in its individuality – Struggle for self-control and power over things and people – Destructive hostility towards all that frustrates desires of the self	– Seeks intelletual and aesthetic satisfaction, honours, titles, prestige – Seeks for love: to unite with others singly or in a group
– More subtle attitudes of dominance and pride – Ascendance of superior personality, subordination of passions to reason, personal autonomy – Effort to establish justice in the world	– Seeks for pure love and friendship – Desire for communication and communion with others according to higher feelings, and in an ever richer intimacy – Desire to understand everything and explain everything
– Subordination of natural powers to the transfiguring action of the Spirit – Self-abnegation, sobriety, obedience – Gentleness, humility, service of others – Attempt to do great things for Christ, to bear trials, transforming suffering through love – To persevere in the faith, fidelity	– Voluntary poverty, abandonment to divine Providence – Desire for eternal things – Personal love of God – Love of others in God, communion with him in his inmost truth, that is to say in Christ and like Christ, even to sacrifice of self – Love of enemies – Enlarging of heart to embrace everyone – Silence before the mystery, solitude in communion – Purity of love, gift of self

who lives in me'. The centre around which our being is organised is henceforth no longer our self but Christ.

At every level there is radical transcendence. Let us go through the list from top to bottom. The great strength of affirmation and aggression that is found in us reaches its paradoxical fulfilment in self-abnegation, obedience, gentleness, humility and forbearance. The lust for possessions ends in the freedom of voluntary poverty, the thirst for knowledge in silence before the mystery, the desire for communion of love in the purity of the total gift of self to the Other.

Such is the end towards which we tend throughout our life. The unfolding of the spiritual life does not suppress the needs of the other levels of our life. We must eat to be able to sing the glory of God. In reality, our life is an integration of all these elements, the lower becoming subordinate to the higher. This is thus not the suppression of natural needs. Our temperament and our personality are the raw material for the work of our sanctification. It is the capital given to each of us. It is a matter of knowing this in all clarity, and taking responsibility for it so that it can be made fruitful. Nothing is bad in this perspective. Even the deepest wounds can be used by grace. In many saints, needs that were there at the outset (for example, in St Bernard, aggression – the need to dominate) were slowly purified and put at the service of the higher values of divine Love, deliberately chosen.

What is essential for each one of us is to know our needs (they vary from person to person) and to find a way to realise them, or a path of purification that is consonant with the values and state of life that we have chosen. The formula will be different for each one and will be subject to revision throughout life. What must be avoided is allowing the existence of unrecognised and repressed needs that look for satisfaction in false guises, contrary to the gospel values to which we want to commit ourselves.

One of the reasons it is so difficult to find and maintain a healthy equilibrium in our life is the limited range of possibilities that it offers for the realisation of human needs. The solitary life necessarily places itself under the sign of the Cross, of a radical transcendence that cannot be fruitful except under the influence of great love. This requires an intense spiritual life and an adequately developed human maturity. We cannot take short cuts with impunity. We can renounce only what we possess, one way or another.

To grasp better the complex reality of the person (and at the price of some repetition), we will first take a synthetic look (see the adjacent tables and try to grasp the movement of transformation that progresses from top to bottom of each column). Then we will look from the angle of psychological maturity.

Here is one way to analyse the two basic impulses:

Aggressive Impulses

healthy	unhealthy
– modest self-affirmation	– exaggerated self-affirmation (often caused by lack of esteem, and feelings of inferiority)
– confronts danger with courage and strength	
– self-control, personal autonomy	– dominating, authoritarian and arrogant attitudes
– attempts difficult things	– hostility towards people who cause frustration, of love above all
– overcomes resistance of body and background by devotion to noble ideals, justice, fraternity, etc.	– 'death-wish', destroyer
– perseveres in effort	
– struggle for virtue	
– transformation of suffering through love	
– self-abnegation	
– gentleness, humility, obedience	
– life of the Spirit	

Libidinal Impulses

Greedy and Possessive		Pleasurable and Erotic	
healthy	*unhealthy*	*healthy*	*unhealthy*
– normal feelings and appetites	– exaggerated greed above all for food and drink	– physical and sexual love	– gluttonous and infantile love:
– curiosity to see and to know	– greed for possessions in the hunger for esteem (vanity), adulation, etc.	– filial and social love	infatuation prostitution nymphomania auto- eroticism sexual deviation sadism masochism
– search for intellectual and aesthetic values		– love of friendship, noble and intimate communion with others	
– desire for eternal things		– love of enemies, of all people in Christ	
– voluntary poverty		– love of God	
– abandonment to divine Providence of God		– solitude in communion	
– silence before the mystery		– gift of self	
		– chastity, purity of love	

19

Psychological Maturity

It is interesting to consider those attitudes that psychology (without making moral judgement) considers maladaptive or adaptive, solely from the perspective of the integration of the personality and human maturity. It is understood that the Christian is called to something more – but not to something less. We do not have the right to neglect this humble level of human reality. Too often the spiritual life is weakened by lack of groundwork at the human level.

MALADAPTIVE ATTITUDES[1]

1. *Ambivalent and vacillating attitudes* that begin to form in infancy and manifest themselves in hesitations, doubts, scruples, compulsions and phobias, and also in certain forms of unbelief and religious scepticism, in certain forms of duplicity related to hysteria.
2. *Hostile attitudes* that spring from a person's spontaneous aggression and also from other factors that manifest themselves in anger, violence against others and self, sharp words and calumny, paranoia, resentment, hate.
3. *Arrogant attitudes* that are another form of aggression tending to dominate others and to believe the self superior to them. These manifest themselves through tyranny and insubordination, contempt and self-complacency.
4. *Greedy and possessive attitudes* through which the individual seeks satisfaction through food and drink, often to compensate for other deprivations, or through which he

is led to appropriate various objects, by deceit or theft, which are not always used, but which are desired for the pleasure of possession.

5. *Pleasure-seeking and affective attitudes* that look for legitimate satisfaction but also for the abuse of sexual pleasure and the deviations that go with it.

6. *Defensive attitudes* in which the person cannot engage life without reservation but is defensive, as in many forms of deceit, hysteria, duplicity, hypocrisy, phony excuses (conscious or unconscious), reaction formation.[2]

7. *Regressive attitudes* in which an individual does not engage in active defensiveness but lapses into inertia, with feelings of inferiority, accompanied by timidity, melancholy, stereotyped behaviour, schizoid behaviour and depressive states in general.

8. *Attitudes of evasion and compensation* through which those who have failed to find inner harmony seek to obtain, on another plane and sometimes in the imaginary world, the satisfactions which they cannot find either in work or in the real world.

ADAPTIVE ATTITUDES

A. IN REGARD TO SELF

1. *Emotional self-control* without rigidity or violence. Through slow labour to have mastery over the emotions by avoiding dramatising situations and by persuading oneself that a sustained effort, animated by a high ideal, enables quicker progress than alternating between violence against oneself and indifference.

2. *Constancy in pursuit of professed goals* which are determined through reflection, wise deliberation and free

choice. To know how to organise one's energy in service of these goals without feeling overwhelmed by them.

3. *The capacity to enlarge one's point of view* through honest encounter with those of others, without passion or obstinacy, and, if it is appropriate, to accept being questioned, to relinquish a point of view formerly held.

4. *Objectivity in judgements*, that is to say, knowing how to evaluate according to their true value the disparate factors, reasons and motives that enter into right judgement (in contrast with judgement that is rash, easily led, impassioned).

5. *To know how to take responsibility for one's actions*, to accept their consequences without using other people or things as scapegoats.

6. *To have the will to draw on one's own resources* with courage, to the fullest extent possible, in the face of difficulties yet without rejecting the help that one can receive from others.

B. WITH REGARD TO THE WORLD AND TO OTHERS

7. *To maintain a healthy balance between introversion and extroversion.* Not to be too withdrawn, cut off from concrete reality; or superficial, without an interior life, restless and unstable. The balance between these two extremes varies according to temperament and the circumstances of life. With the contemplative, introversion is habitually dominant.

We must know how to go out of ourselves to relate to things and other people, and also how to come back into ourselves. We must know how to relate to others without being completely swamped by them. True presence to others presupposes a real presence within ourselves that seeks to understand from within what the other wants to communicate.

8. *Accepting others*, the condition of any social life. Almost all neurosis is a form of intolerance of others and provokes reactions that are aggressive, fearful, egotistical, deceitful, etc. We must accept others with all their limitations and shortcomings. We all have them.

9. *To accept others' criticisms and suggestions.*

10. *The capacity to face unforeseen situations and misfortune*; to respond to an obstacle by renewed efforts to transcend it; to begin again without looking back and without recrimination, in a courageous and constructive way.

PARTICULAR TRAITS OF CHRISTIAN MATURITY

Let us lengthen the psychological lens to a properly Christian focus. The law of Christ is summarised in love of God and neighbour. This presupposes the qualities specified above but goes farther in the sense of a love that is more universal and more true. The virtues that Christ requires are precisely those that are most opposed to human egoism and that promote unity among people.

– Against the appeal of sensuality, Christ sets a chastity that bonds people at a level that is both the most universal and the most personal, and calls for a complete gift of self in love.

– Against the appeal of violence, Christ sets meekness, gentleness, mutual forgiveness and love of enemies, the foundation of all true peace.

– Against the rampant desire for riches and pride at the expense or in contempt of others, Christ sets voluntary poverty, freedom from covetousness (freedom to love), humble obedience, affective solidarity with the poor and weak, humility.

– Against deceit in all its forms, hypocrisy, Christ sets the
simplicity of open trust with humans and God, transparency in the light of a sincerity that accepts clearly what
we are – sinners – and accepts others.

PSYCHOLOGICAL MATURITY IN THE CONTEXT
OF RELIGIOUS LIFE

Let us try to apply the essence of these gifts to the monk
within the concrete framework of his life. But it must be said
that this will be a very idealised monk!

ATTITUDES TOWARDS ONESELF

It is fundamental to have a healthy acceptance of oneself as
one truly is, to have confidence in one's ability to face life,
to possess a certain personal security. This can be more or
less facilitated by personal aptitude and life experience, but
in the final analysis, in every case, this must rest on faith in
the personal love of God for each of us in Christ, and on
faith in the power of the Holy Spirit to transfigure us.

The mature monk lives in the world as it is: he does not
need to distort his perception as a defence against unresolved
interior conflicts. He accepts the clearly perceived legitimate
needs of his nature and temperament and integrates them
with the values of his vocation: he is himself in all simplicity.

Because his energy is not sapped by struggling to resolve
interior conflicts, he can deal with the tensions that arise
from the renunciation attendant on religious life, the lack
of reference points in solitude and the relative absence of
reflection of himself to himself by another person which
solitude entails. He can deal also with unexpected circumstances and the inevitable trials. He shows a certain consistency in attitude that does not obviate the deepening that
comes with experience.

ATTITUDES TOWARDS OTHERS

Having self-confidence, he has a fundamental confidence in others. His relationship with others contains a minimum of anxiety and hostility (as when others are perceived as a threat). He loves them in an unselfish way, in Christ, for who they are, not for what they have, without seeking ego gratification.

His relationship with superiors is characterised neither by dependence nor independence but by dependability and responsibility. He assumes the exigencies of obedience without feeling humiliated and without diminishment of responsibility and initiative.

ATTITUDE IN REGARD TO VOCATIONAL VALUES

He has freely and personally chosen the values and assumed the obligations of his vocation because they are in harmony with his basic values, with what he has integrated in his personal belief system. He neither rebels on principle nor blindly and anxiously conforms with the established norms of the life. (The two reactions arise from the same psychological mechanism. Both unconsciously use the fact of being a member of an Order not to actualise the spiritual values of an authentic personal ideal, but as a defence against his incompatible needs (unconscious) and as a partial resolution of his deepest frustration.)

He does not identify his personal security with exterior structures and observances, and he does not feel threatened when they are called into question or changed.

He distinguishes between what is essential and what is accidental, between the compromise of principle and compromise at the level of concrete action. He respects the diversity of personal graces.

He shows flexibility and realism in the concrete expression

of the values of his vocation, avoiding fantasy as much as excessive rigidity.

He is clear-eyed in his acceptance of the restriction of his personal liberty implied by belonging to a group. He places himself in the school of tradition while remaining faithful to his individual grace.

ATTITUDES TOWARDS GOD

He knows how to pass beyond parental and other models of God in order to cast himself into the Mystery of his Love revealed in Christ; to allow himself to be loved and to be rendered capable of loving in his turn, a love without fear but not without reverence, free, confident and filial.

To pray is a vital necessity for him; to adore, the spontaneous movement of his being; to obey, a duty of love; to be open to the Light, his joy.

Truth, peace, liberty, love.

APPENDIX

THE 'JOHARI' WINDOW

	self-knowledge	lack of self-knowledge
known by others	public self	blind self
not known by others	hidden self	unknown or under-developed potential

Teaching Note

Let us not be discouraged if we have to admit our lack of maturity on any particular point, and recognise that we are far from the ideal described. As we have already said, maladaptive attitudes are not necessarily defects in the moral sense.

They are rather an expression of our wounds and weaknesses. We would like to be and act in all things in the image of Christ, in Love.

The human person grows into maturity only through a sustained effort that often lasts throughout life. Sometimes there are certain deprivations and wounds in our history, above all from childhood, which are incorporated into the structure of our personality and which can never entirely be healed, but only accepted.

There are also attitudes that can be modified through a suitable educational programme. This effort must be prudent, progressive and sustained. In the beginning there must be a *clear-eyed understanding* of the virtue that is sought or the defective attitude that is to be redirected. It requires a resolute will to accomplish this (purity of intention). But this is not enough. Without a progressive and sustained effort to bring instinctual and affective life into harmony with the demands of the spirit, there is a risk of one's responses remaining wishful thinking. There must be *regular training*, that is to say, repeated ascetic exercises, forming good habits that re-order mental processes, that establish control over impulses and muscles, that facilitate the willed attitude. Practice makes perfect and for this there must be time and patience.

But there is also a very real danger. An asceticism that is only of the will risks creating a set of rigid automatic responses that dictate behaviour and prevent the individual from adapting to new situations in life and the variables with which he is confronted. In addition, the temptation is as great for the teacher as for the individual to hasten the process by challenging behaviour with additional threats, shocks and humiliation, punishments, things more alienating still than the normally acquired routines – especially in the context of the religious life where the sanctions have a 'sacred' character.

In this way, deliberately acquired (and necessary)

responses risk imprisoning and alienating the spirit, instead of being in its service. To avoid this it is important to mediate the process through the affective, which adds to the good will, the positive disposition of the feelings towards the demands of the spirit. It must take the heart into consideration which, through either resistance or co-operation, can obstruct or facilitate the virtuous endeavour by involving the energy of the whole person.

To unblock a frustrated or damaged affectivity so that it can be involved in the effort that the spirit must make with regard to the instincts, and so to enable the acquisition of desired habits – this is often the meaning of the re-education that all conversion requires.

The monk should try to let himself be seduced by the beauty of his vocation: God's beauty first of all, but also the beauty of his daily life in all its dimensions, human and aesthetic. He ought to seek to love his duty. Love is more effective than a rigid and austere law administered principally by prohibitions and imposed from the 'outside'. Love makes us happier, kinder and more flexible before the demands that come to us from others, and from changing circumstances.

As far as possible, the heart should be mobilised in the service of that which we want to love. The consent of our affectivity is essential for the unity of the person. Without it we risk maintaining a certain duplicity in our behaviour, ambivalences, resistances; to use the force of the will alone renders the ascetic enterprise ineffectual.

For the rest, we must not have any illusions. It is only the 'superior' conscious affectivity that is teachable and can be educated to a certain degree. The 'lower', unconscious affectivity is not subject to reason and is in large measure impenetrable.

20

The Great Journey

Two among you will soon take the habit. Both have travelled far in their search for God. We can look at their next step from this angle. Let us talk of the great journey that is opening before them.

Once more let us plunge ourselves into some pericopes of St Luke (9:51–62): this one presents the central part of Jesus' public mission as a great journey towards Jerusalem. So first of all, let us trace this theme in the whole Gospel.

The first part of the Gospel according to St Luke describes the birth and the advent of Jesus, the Word of grace in the Holy Spirit, then the gathering of disciples around Jesus (1:5—4:44), who is more or less recognised as Messiah in his signs of power and in his words (4:45—9:17). Every gaze is fixed on him in the hope of a longed-for salvation.

Then a new time is ushered in (9:18—17:10). From this time onwards, the person of Jesus no longer monopolises attention, he becomes as one who is taken gradually away from his own, making his way to the Father at the same time that he goes up to Jerusalem. He makes himself more and more 'a reference to the Father', 'the revelation of the Father', 'the promise of the Spirit'. His itinerary and ours are not in essence spatial, but spiritual.

Prayer, interiority, take a greater and greater place, even as the mystery of the intimacy of Jesus is revealed to those who follow him. It is a matter of recognising which Spirit he is, and which Father he obeys on his way towards Jerusalem, and of inviting his disciples to accompany him, to follow him, in an obedience that mirrors his own.

Thus Jesus opens us to the mystery of the Kingdom of God (chs. 9—13) and its gratuity (chs. 14—17). To engage oneself with Jesus is not a work on a human scale: it can only be received as a grace. Let us look a little at this process. Let us listen first of all to Christ.

Once when Jesus was praying alone, with only the disciples near him, he asked them, 'Who do the crowds say that I am?' They answered, 'John the Baptist; but others, Elijah; and still others, that one of the ancient prophets has arisen.' He said to them, 'But who do you say that I am?' Peter answered, 'The Messiah of God.'
He sternly ordered and commanded them not to tell anyone, saying, 'The Son of Man must undergo great suffering, and be rejected by the elders, chief priests, and scribes, and be killed, and on the third day be raised.'
Then he said to them all, 'If any want to become my followers, let them deny themselves and take up their cross daily and follow me. For those who want to save their life will lose it, and those who lose their life for my sake will save it. What does it profit them if they gain the whole world, but lose or forfeit themselves? Those who are ashamed of me and of my words, of them the Son of Man will be ashamed, when he comes in his glory and the glory of the Father and of the holy angels. But truly I tell you, there are some standing here who will not taste death before they see the kingdom of God.' (Luke 9:18–27)

'While Jesus was praying' (9:18). The interior dimension of his being is clarified. 'Who am I?' for the crowd, for the disciples. Prayer places him in the presence of the Father, it is his existence with and for the Father. His identity as Son is established through relationship to the Father and cannot be rightly seen apart from that.
Peter proclaims him 'Christ of God', Messiah. But to go

to the extremity of his act of faith will be to be seized in prayer, to be taken up, 'making his way' to the Father.

Entry into the mystery of the person of Jesus begins with the revelation of the destiny that awaits him: the Passion and Resurrection. This destiny is placed under the sign of prayer (v. 18); thus its emphasis is less on the necessity of dying than on the way to the Father. Faced with this necessity ('he must'), even the attitude of the disciples is required to change. It is not merely conversion to Jesus. It is the commitment to follow him to the Father: 'Come, follow me' (9:23). This passage (Easter) to the Father is a trial for each one, a radical transcendence.

To share the destiny of Jesus in going to the Father requires self-denial, to carry our cross each day. This denial is not resignation, a refusal to be ourselves; it is to receive our life as a grace on which we never close our hand, and each day to endure the struggle of our fragile powers of love and freedom against the hurtful forces in us and around us. We cannot save our life as we save our skin, in seeking to withdraw into ourselves, or to escape suffering and death at any price. It is rather in going out to meet them. It is a matter of abandoning all self-sufficiency in order to find in Jesus our sole reason for living, our only hope for justice, for love, for life.

What end does it serve if we conquer success or power, if it is the fruit of personal ambition, a ruinous and definitive bondage? It is for the disciple to follow the master through the trial of temptation and find salvation in him, abandoning all attempts to dominate. The eternal truth of what we live here below will be unveiled in the face of the Son of Man and of the Father and of the holy angels.

And this mysterious promise: 'There are some standing here who will not taste death before they see the kingdom of God' (v. 27): this does not say that they will escape physical death, but more likely means that in the present suffering endured for Jesus, they will taste the power of his risen life. The verb 'to see' suggests this hidden participation in the life of the resurrection, which is mystical contemplation. This promise should be realised at least by some of those who are called to the contemplative life. 'Taste and see how gracious the Lord is.'

The episode of the Transfiguration lifts a corner of the veil that conceals the mystery of the 'Christ of God'. To Peter, James and John, enfolded by the prayer of Jesus, it is given to see him in glory in the company of Moses and Elijah. The two men speak with Jesus of his 'exodus',[1] which he will accomplish in Jersusalem. The term 'exodus' evokes the liberation from Egypt under the leadership of Moses, and that is why he is present. Later (v. 51) the text speaks of his being 'taken up', recalling Elijah's ascension to God to reappear in the days of the Messiah (2 Kings 2:9–11), and this is why the prophet too is here.

Jerusalem is named as the destination. From now on it focuses every aspect of Jesus' life: he goes there to be with his Father.

Even as a boy he knew he should be with his Father (2:49); he was loved by him from eternity. The meaning of his earthly 'making his way' is to go up to the Father – this is the translation of his prayer into history, his face, his filial being turned towards the Father.

The mystery of this way escapes human understanding, and Peter's proposal to build three dwellings falls on its face. It is not the part of human beings, it is not our part to build a shelter for God through the efforts of our 'virtue' or through the inventions of our intellect. God himself overshadows us with his presence, as with Mary at the annunciation (1:35). Instinctively we are afraid, we are out of our depth. We know that to see God is to die (Judges 6:22–3). But this is the revelation: the person whom Jesus brings with him is taken into the cloud and receives a share in the divine intimacy. We must therefore go with him, up with him to Jerusalem, go up with the Servant of God to face his agony.

Then, a little further on (9:51) Jesus sets himself definitively on the way: 'When the days drew near for him to be taken up, he set his face to go to Jerusalem.' The word 'face' expresses both this person's determination and his being turned towards the goal, that is, towards the Father.

For our part, let us set our own faces. The way will be hard, and we must not allow ourselves to be sidetracked by its difficulties. We must have an absolute determination; come what may, we must not give up. As I have frequently said: to persevere in the Charterhouse, this willingness must be uncompromising; there is always, for each of us, at one time or another, a moment which presents a 'reasonable' and legitimate reason for leaving this way . . .

The presence of Jesus making his way towards Jerusàlem effects a discernment of hearts. The Samaritans shunned him just because of his destination. It has been the same throughout history. This often will be the case for us. But we should not be afraid. The judgement Jesus bears is not a judgement of condemnation. James and John, wanting to call down fire from heaven, were rebuked (9:54–6). Instead, Jesus brings the judgement of forgiveness and mercy (23:34). He wills to fulfil, not destroy, to save, not to lose.

Three short scenes let us see what this signifies concretely: to follow Jesus to the Father: 'As they were going along the road, someone said to him, "I will follow you wherever you go." And Jesus said to him, "Foxes have holes, and birds of the air have nests; but the son of Man has nowhere to lay his head" ' (9:57–8). After his birth at Bethlehem and now more than ever, Jesus leads the life of a stranger, a sojourner. The disciples will be given up to the same adventure of poverty and insecurity.

'To another he said, "Follow me." But he said, "Lord, first let me go and bury my father." But Jesus said to him,

"Let the dead bury their own dead; but as for you, go and proclaim the kingdom of God" ' (9:59–60). This time it is Jesus who takes the initiative. What did he read in this man's heart? Good will, but timidity. He must shake him up a little. The man asks for a delay; in fact, the filial duty of piety laid on a Jew the obligation to ensure the burial of his parents (Genesis 50:5, etc.). Jesus' reply is intransigent. The Kingdom has priority even over this obligation, however sacred it might be (cf. Luke 14:26). Life comes before death. Besides, the care of the dead is much less important in the light of the promise of eternal life.

The third scene, like the first, tells of a man who offered himself: ' "I will follow you, Lord; but let me first say farewell to those at my home." Jesus said to him, "No one who puts a hand to the plow and looks back[2] is fit for the kingdom of God" ' (9:61–2). The man states only one condition, and it seems very reasonable. In an analogous situation, Elisha, equally involved in his work, is called to prophetic ministry by Elijah, who throws his mantle over him; Elisha asks, 'Let me kiss my father and my mother, and then I will follow you' (1 Kings 19:20). And Elijah lets him. But Jesus does not. The last days have dawned, the time of final decision, the *kairos*. Entry into the Kingdom will not allow for delay. Who knows if the grace offered today will be there tomorrow? Above all it will not allow anyone to look back.

At the age of twelve, Jesus focused his parents' attention towards the Father when they came looking for him in the temple (Luke 2:49). His attitude has not changed; it becomes even more urgently expressed to whoever wishes to follow him in his 'exodus-taking up'. The disciple of Jesus has but one concern: 'Forgetting what lies behind and straining forward to what lies ahead . . . [he] press[es] on toward the goal for the prize of the heavenly[3] call of God in Christ Jesus' (Philippians 3:13–14).

Perhaps a psychological reading can show in this threefold

renunciation the break with the image of the mother (symbol of exterior security, of the comfort of the home), with the image of the father (representing the religion of obligation: you must do this and you will be in order, in security, before the demands of God, of Love), and with the familiar ties and the burden of constraint, and all of this in the service of the goal of being authentic, adult, free to follow Christ in the adventure of Love's gratuitousness.

In every way, the call addressed to the disciple invites him to enter into the prayer of the Son, to become a son, to turn with all his being towards the Father, and here and now to break the shackles that tie down his little ego. He is invited to allow himself to be taken up by the Father, to leave everything to find life eternal, the heart of the Father. 'I want to know Christ and the power of his resurrection and the sharing of his sufferings by becoming like him in his death, if somehow I may attain the resurrection from the dead' (Philippians 3:10–11).

Jesus has completed his own journey and is seated at the right hand of the Father. Nonetheless, he does not leave us to make our way alone. Living, he is with us. The story of Emmaus well illustrates his presence (Luke 24:13–32).

After his death, two of the disciples were on their way to a village called Emmaus. They turned their backs to Jerusalem. Sad and discouraged, they understood nothing of what had happened. All their hopes were lost. Nevertheless, they speak of what they have seen and, in effect, find themselves with the material of the proclamation of the resurrection of Christ on the third day: the women's story, the absence of the body, the vision of angels, the testimony of their companions. But they can find no coherence in these events. They do not see. The key is not available to them. A stranger approaches and walks along with them. At first he listens in silence, then he opens them to the spirit of the Word of God; he makes them understand everything that had happened. God's plan rises before them like a vital necessity. 'Was it not necessary . . . ?' This recapitulates the first word of the child Jesus in the temple (Luke 2:49). Finally the disciples understand. Their hearts burn in them because the word of Jesus bears the Spirit, the fire that he has come to kindle on the earth (Luke 12:49). He heals their heart, he awakens faith in hearts 'slow to believe' (Luke 24:25).

Thus it is sometimes for us. We do not understand the meaning of what we live, the meaning of our way through our life. Then, one day, light shines through the Word and the Spirit. It was necessary . . . It was necessary that Christ suffered this – it is Christ who suffers, who makes his way with us even to the end of the world to enter into his glory.

They approach the village and Jesus acts as if he would continue on. He is, in fact, going to make us penetrate into our faith more deeply. Faith is not nourished by words alone but also through a presence. 'Stay with us . . . ' and he went in and stayed with them. Then, 'he took bread, blessed and broke it, and gave it to them' (Luke 24:30). The bread of temptation in the desert, the bread of the Father that must be asked for, the bread that Jesus shares with sinners, with the Pharisees, with his friends, is the bread of his Body given, enabling our lives to be communion with his life, because he chooses to sit at table with us.

'Then their eyes were opened and they recognised him' (Luke 24:31). Jesus' presence is recognised at precisely this moment. 'He vanished from their sight.' He disappears as a tangible, visible presence, to become a transparency of what they are living: the bread shared with a neighbour, the memorial-gesture of his sacrifice that makes him present. The risen One is there, living but invisible, in the elements of the broken bread but also in the elements and appearances of their everyday existence. When we were far off, Jesus perhaps made himself near, almost visible to us. But now that our faith is more enlightened, he leads us into a more interior presence of faith: presence of his humanity in the Eucharist and other sacraments, presence in the Church, in the broken bread of a life daily shared with our brothers. Because it is together that we make our way to the Father.

> There are already two of you; walk with us, and
> *bon voyage*!

> When the Lord delivered Zion from bondage,
> It seemed like a dream.
> Then was our mouth filled with laughter,
> on our lips there were songs.
>
> The heathens themselves said: 'What marvels
> the Lord worked for them!'
> What marvels the Lord worked for us!
> Indeed we were glad.
>
> Deliver us, O Lord, from our bondage
> as streams in dry land.
> Those who are sowing in tears
> will sing when they reap.
>
> They go out, they go out, full of tears,
> carrying seed for the sowing:
> They come back, they come back, full of song,
> carrying their sheaves.
> Psalm 125[4] (Grail version, Vulgate numbering)

Notes

CHAPTER 1: **Bruno: A Time, a Place, a Man**

1 Augustine, *City of God*, XI, 24.

CHAPTER 2: **The Statutes**

1 Statutes numbers in this volume are keyed to the 1993 Statutes.

2 An allusion to a remark attributed variously to Bernard, William, or Ivo of Chartres, but in any case enshrined in the windows of the south transept of Chartres cathedral.

3 See the *Fontes Statutorum*, pp. 1–3; *L'Ordre des Chartreux*, pp. 25 and 26, the appendix at the end of this conference.

4 See *La Grande Chartreuse par un Chartreux* (1976 edition), pp. 150–6, and the conciliar decree *Perfectae Caritatis*, 2, 3, 7, 9 etc.

5 In practical terms, this is not easy. Carthusians are always more eager to live their lives than to write history, There is a lack of documentation. One important work of scholarly history was written in this century by Dom Maurice Laporte: *Aux Origines de la Vie Cartusienne*. See also *Les Ephémérides* of Dom Le Vasseur and the *Annales* of Dom Le Couteulx, both from the seventeenth century. These are good historical works (in Latin) of their time, but we are far from the sources. There are also numerous monographs on particular houses and notable personalities. But we lack a satisfactory history of the Order as a whole.

CHAPTER 3: **Vocation**

1 Abraham (Genesis 12:1–5); Moses (Exodus 3 and 4); Samuel (1 Samuel 3); David (1 Samuel 16:1–13); Isaiah (Isaiah 6); Jeremiah (Jeremiah 1); the Servant (Isaiah 41:8–14; 42:1–9; 49:1–6; 50:4–9; 52:13—53:12); Mary (Luke 1:26–38); the first disciples (John 1:35–51); Peter (John 21:15–19); the young man (Matthew 19:16–22); Paul (Galatians 1:15–16; Acts 9) etc.

2 Translator's note: The transparent beauty and subtlety of this conference is too easily lost in translation. Thus all of the words marked

* are translations of the French word *sein*, which can mean breast,
bosom, heart, midst, womb, gulf, depth, and is used in association
with both Abraham and the Virgin Mary. Words marked † are
translations of the French word *dessein*, meaning design, plan, purpose, view, or (freely) in reference to God, something that proceeds
from the divine heart.

3 Consider the corresponding passages: Isaiah 40:3, 6–8 and John 1:1;
Isaiah 52:6 and John 1:14; Isaiah 55:11 and John 16:28, 17:26 and
19:30.

4 Our personal vocation, in so far as we have it in common with all
Christians, but also specifically through our call to Carthusian life.
We should not hesitate to distinguish the universal call and the
particular call, nor the commandments and the counsels. Our perspective will become that of concrete and unified reality.

CHAPTER 4: The Call

1 Translator's note: In French, literally, 'through faithfulness I draw
you to myself'.

2 Revelation gives us all the reasons that there are to love God. Here
it is a question of something more radical, analogous to the spontaneous and irresistible attraction between one person and another,
which precedes all reasoning and all justification. In essence, it is
the work of God's love poured out in our hearts (Romans 5:5); and,
in us, too, love has no why.

3 *Confessions*, X, 6.

4 See the poem by Francis Thompson, 'The hound of heaven'.

5 Jeremiah 11:18–23; 12:1–6; 15:10; 15:20; 17:14–18; 18:18–23;
20:17–18.

6 Perseverance in a state of life frequently depends on the strength of
these hidden (hidden even from us) and selfish motives. A vocation
which is predominantly motivated by this sort of human expectation
(social prestige, self-affirmation, search for a refuge from too harsh
a reality, etc.) will be shaken if and when these expectations are not
fulfilled.

CHAPTER 5: Sell Everything That You Have

1 Compare the response of Zacchaeus, the rich sinner, to the call of
Christ (Luke 19:1–10).

2 According to certain theologians, at this instant we are given the

possibility of an act chosen in full clarity before the glorified Christ. All of our being is unified and possesses the 'full likeness' and will be finally committed. This act will determine our eternity, because we will choose, in complete clarity and definitive fashion, like the angels, to accept or refuse the love of God in Christ. This choice will be the fruit of our whole life. The only way for us to be certain that we will choose life, love, Christ, is to choose them now during our life in the world.

3 One could quote any mystic on this point. For example, John of the Cross: 'To attain all you must renounce all. And when you come to possess all, you must possess wanting nothing. Because if you want to have something in the all, your treasure is not purely God.'

CHAPTER 6: Follow Me

1 Let us stay with the Synoptics for a moment. We will look at St John's narrative later.

2 St Thomas Aquinas, *Summa Theologiae*, III, 1, Q. 48, a. 5, ad. 3.

3 Excerpts from the Decree on the Adaptation and Renewal of Religious Life, *Perfectae caritatis*, 1, 2. See W. M. Abbott SJ, *The Documents of Vatican II* (London: Geoffrey Chapman, 1967), pp. 466–8.

CHAPTER 7: You Will See

1 Translator's note: This is how the French translates the Hebrew. The NIV literal translation is 'they-will-see to eye-eye-for they-shout-for-joy people-of-him'. See John R. Kohlenberger III (ed.), *The NIV Interlinear Hebrew–English Old Testament* (Grand Rapids, Regency), p. 107.

2 See also St Paul: 'For it is the God who said, "Let light shine out of darkness", who has shone in our hearts to give the light of the knowledge of the glory of God in the face of Jesus Christ' (2 Corinthians 4:6). '. . . He is the image [icon] of the invisible God . . .' (Colossians 1:15).

3 This seems to be the best translation of this phrase – see Boismard, *Ev. de S. Jean*, p. 358, note Y in the TOB, p. 332, and the English NRSV.

4 cf. *The Way of Silent Love*, Sixth Conference.

5 Examples of this in human relationships are not lacking: for example, being together in silence, we understand without exterior signs;

or being united precisely in absence or beyond death. Translator's note: See the Anglo-Saxon poem *The Wanderer* for a poignant account, and for a biblical overview of this theme, see Samuel Terrien's *The Elusive Presence* (New York: Harper and Row, 1978).

6 See also St Paul: 'And all of us, with unveiled faces, seeing the glory of the Lord as though reflected in a mirror, are being transformed into the same image from one degree of glory to another; for this comes from the Lord, the Spirit' (2 Corinthians 3:18).

7 The commentators are not in agreement as to his identity: probably it was John, but Lazarus has his advocates, too, etc.

CHAPTER 9: **The School of the Holy Spirit**
1 There are others: we will look at them later.

CHAPTER 10: **The Interior Master**

1 The somewhat crude modern experiments on psychosomatic or mental techniques and drugs at least have had the advantage of proving the existence of other forms of consciousness, which are suppressed in the majority of people but which are ready to be awakened by the appropriate stimulus.

2 Even at the level of natural psychology this image is merely a convenient simplification of a highly complex reality.

3 In the structure of the intellect, there are two principal forms of resistance to the light of the Spirit: first, excessive attachment to purely rational insight, rationalism in all its forms, with the consequent distrust of any light that is not purely rational; pride and intellectual self-sufficiency; second, superficiality or lack of attentiveness to spiritual realities. Both can be found in hidden form in the Charterhouse.

4 William of St Thierry, *The Golden Epistle*, 16: 'It is for others to serve God, it is for you to cling to him; it is for others to believe in God, know him, love him and revere him; it is for you to taste him, understand him, be acquainted with him, enjoy him. This is no slight matter, no easy goal.' Translated by Theodore Berkeley ocso (Kalamazoo: Cistercian Publications, 1976), p. 14.

5 ibid., 256–63, with some retranslation.

CHAPTER 11: **The Discernment of Spirits**

1 According to Paul prophecy is, under the influence of the Holy Spirit, a gift of succour through speech. This gift completes and enables discernment of spirits. From another point of view, it is completed by the discernment, because it can happen that someone mingles with words inspired by the Spirit things drawn from within himself and blurred by error. To distinguish the divine and the human, there is then need of discernment.

2 The power of the Spirit can be shown in hidden works of humility, prayer, the testing of faith in solitude, etc.

3 Translator's note: the word 'light' is in the French and is essential to the discussion; most English translations use the word 'knowledge'.

4 Translator's note: The French is 'la Parole'.

CHAPTER 12: **Discernment of Spirits in Monastic Tradition**

1 See L. Bouyer, *La Vie de S. Antoine*; Evagrius Ponticus, *The Praktikos*; Cassian, especially *Conferences*, II, V and VII; *Dict. Spir.*, 'Démon', 'Discernement des esprits', etc.

2 Cassian, *Conferences*, II, 2.

3 Judgement does not necessarily go hand in hand with 'culture'. A peasant without training can have good judgement. In certain cases, if there is a minimum of real ability, it is possible through slow pedagogical work to free judgement from certain vices, above all if they arise from emotional pressures which, in principle, are curable.

4 It seems that in the actual circumstances in which many novices become 'converts', their faith is without roots in the family or community; thus a new importance and/or special role falls on the little community of novices which has to assimilate, and, partly, to form, its new members.

5 Cassian, *Conferences*, II, 4.

6 Cassian, *Conferences*, II, 10.

CHAPTER 13: **The Purification of the Passions**

1 Evagrius, *Praktikos*, Prologue, 8.

2 It seems that it was Evagrius who systematised the expression of the first Fathers in this way. Cassian (cf. his Fifth Conference) and later tradition follow his enumeration and it is the source of our list of the seven deadly sins.

3 Sometimes translated 'melancholy'. The author wishes to make a

distinction between an habitual or constitutional tendency to sadness, a melancholic temperament, which is predisposed by nature to fall into this passion for which he prefers the word 'sadness'.

4 Thoughts suggested by the demon of gluttony. This is what Evagrius compiled in the fourth century. They are just as applicable today. 'Whether or not the soul is troubled or untroubled by thoughts does not depend on us. Whether they are entertained or not, or whether the passions are unleashed or not – this depends on us.'

5 A normal appetite can grow excessive (bulimia) or, on the other hand, can markedly diminish (anorexia) because of psychological illness: a state of frustrated affectivity that is prolonged and insidious.

6 Note that for the other vices, social life is not harmful; quite the reverse: it helps to correct them. They are more exposed in human exchanges; and even as they manifest themselves more frequently on such occasions, social interchange also affords more rapid healing.

7 One should not 'enter into a discussion' with these temptations, above all those against chastity, nor try to struggle with them directly, which can only result in reinforcing them by focusing attention on them. When one becomes aware that such a thought is present, one should calmly and deliberately (without panic or fear) reject it and turn one's attention to thoughts or activities that are good and absorbing.

8 P. Cruchon SJ, *Initiation à la Psychologie Dynamique*, pp. 55–6.

9 ibid.

CHAPTER 14: **The Purification of the Passions II**

1 'If your brother irritates you, do not hesitate to go to him and to invite him to your house, and eat your bread with him, because in this way your soul will be set free and you will not have any hindrances at the time of your prayer' (Evagrius, *Monks*, 15).

2 This is the anti-rhetorical method that displaces bad thoughts with an appropriate word of Scripture.

3 Trans. Robert T. Meyer (New York, Newman Press).

CHAPTER 15: **The Purification of the Passions III**

1 Se croire un personnage est fort commun en France.
   On y fait l'homme d'importance,
   et l'on n'est souvent qu'un bourgeois:
   c'est proprement le mal français.

La sotte vanite nous es particulière
Les Espagnols sont vains, mais d'une autre manière.
Leur orgueil me semble, en un mot,
beaucoup plus fou, mais pas si sot.
(La Fontaine)

2 A. de Saint-Exupéry, *The Little Prince*, trans. Katherine Woods (London: Pan, 1974), pp. 40–2.

3 cf. George Herbert, 'Teach me, my God and King'.

4 There are concrete descriptions of arrogant novices in Cassian (*Institutes*, XII, 27) that show that human nature has not changed much since his time. Above all, the novice who has an ear for rebellion against the teaching of the master. Throughout the conferences, the novice is restless, as if he were sitting on sharp thorns.

5 Which in its psychotic form is paranoia.

6 See the Rule of St Benedict; the twelve degrees of pride opposed to the twelve degrees of humility of St Bernard; the four degrees of St Gregory in the *Moralia*.

7 cf. *The Ascetical Homilies of Isaac the Syrian*, trans. Dana Miller (Boston: Holy Transfiguration Monastery), pp. 244–5; Bedjan 346.

8 Look for these texts in the Bible. See Cassian, *Institutes*, XI, 4.

9 James Houston (ed.), *The Mind on Fire* (London: Hodder and Stoughton, 1991), p. 157, #188.

10 ibid., p. 151, #175.

11 cf. *Ascetical Homilies*, p. 381; Bedjan 574.

CHAPTER 16: **The Purification of the Passions IV**

1 Isaac the Syrian, *Ascetical Homilies*, p. 154; Bedjan 214.

2 All of this can seem very subtle and complicated to the beginner. In fact, generally speaking, it should only be necessary to apply a particular counsel to the appropriate weak point with an eye to personal history. It is one thing to know how to drive a new car, and quite another to know how to drive a used car and how to fix it.

3 Isaac the Syrian, *Ascetical Homilies*, p. 85. This homily exists only in Greek.

CHAPTER 17: **Discernment of Spirits in Later Tradition**

1 De Guilbert, *Leçons de Théologie Spirituelle*, p. 307.

2 Rightly understood, when it is a matter of applying these rules to our own conduct, the most elementary prudence requires recourse

to the advice of an experienced director. All the signs of a 'doubtful' spirit can be found in a good spirit in certain circumstances.

3 In the same way, we distinguish between objective holiness (the exterior activity of a person) and subjective holiness: interior conformity of the will to grace through love.

CHAPTER 19: **Psychological Maturity**

1 See G. Cruchon SJ, *Initiation à une Psychologie Dynamique*, t. 2, pp. 94 and 95.

2 'False' behaviour that seeks to repress blindly or brutally violent impulses which are not admitted at the conscious level: for example, exaggerated anxiety that masks strong aggression.

CHAPTER 20: **The Great Journey**

1 In the Greek text.

2 The French here inserts 'unceasingly'. (Translator's note)

3 Greek: 'upward'. (Translator's note)

4 The psalms of the Little Hours of Tuesday through Saturday are the psalms of the pilgrims who go up to Jerusalem.

O Bonitas!

FOR FURTHER INFORMATION

St Hugh's Charterhouse
Parkminster, Partridge Green
Horsham, Sussex RH13 8EB

Charterhouse of the Transfiguration
Arlington, Vermont 05250
USA